almost KETO

A PRACTICAL APPROACH TO LOSE WEIGHT WITH LESS FAT AND CLEANER KETO FOODS

Aimee Aristotelous and Richard Oliva
Foreword by Dr. Kenneth Akey

Skyhorse Publishing

Skyhorse Publishing books may be purchased in bulk at special discounts for sales promotion, corporate gifts, fund-raising, or educational purposes. Special editions can also be created to specifications. For details, contact the Special Sales Department, Skyhorse Publishing, 307 West 36th Street, 11th Floor, New York, NY 10018 or info@skyhorsepublishing.com.

Skyhorse® and Skyhorse Publishing® are registered trademarks of Skyhorse Publishing, Inc.®, a Delaware corporation.

Visit our website at www.skyhorsepublishing.com.

10 9 8 7 6 5 4 3 2 1

Library of Congress Cataloging-in-Publication Data is available on file.

Photography by Marcel Boldu, and Hair and Makeup by Deisy Da Silva: pages xiii, xv, 21, 65, 253, and 254.

Cover design by Daniel Brount
Cover photo by gettyimages

Print ISBN: 978-1-5107-5006-7
Ebook ISBN: 978-1-5107-5009-8

Printed in China

To our parents, Steve, Norma, Richard, and Dorothy, who taught us the importance of eating our vegetables, as well as a variety of other healthy foods. And to our son, Alex, who reminds us every day how important it is to share our love of real food and good nutrition.

Contents

Foreword

By Dr. Kenneth Akey

Nutrition information is more readily available today than ever before in our history. While this is a good thing, it also can be very confusing to sort through all the advice on how to eat healthy. Should we follow the USDA MyPlate recommendations and eat whole grains, low-fat dairy, and limit added sugars to fifty to seventy-five grams per day? Should we adopt the Paleo diet and eat no grains, no dairy products, and no added sugars? Or should we choose the ketogenic diet and eat mostly fats, including whole-fat dairy, but no grains or added sugars? With all this conflicting advice, how are we to decide what is the best choice when it comes to our health?

In recent years, the ketogenic (keto) diet has helped many people lose weight and improve overall health. The documented, short-term benefits of the ketogenic diet include a variety of positive health outcomes in addition to weight loss, including reduced blood sugar, triglycerides, and LDL (bad) cholesterol and increased HDL (good) cholesterol. Animal studies have also suggested that the diet may have antiaging, anti-inflammatory, and cancer-fighting benefits. When considering the keto protocol, it is important to note that not all fats are created equal. For the best health outcomes, it is essential to select high-quality fats found in whole foods such as avocado, extra-virgin olive oil, nuts, seeds, and wild salmon versus the detrimental fats found in items such as hot dogs, deli meats, hydrogenated oils, and other processed foods.

Despite these promising results, there are still many questions about the keto diet. There are few studies on the long-term (more than six months) effects of following an extremely high-fat diet. Some research suggests that adhering to keto's extremely low-carbohydrate protocol for extended periods of time could result in vitamin and mineral deficiency, because vegetables and fruits must be severely limited. In addition, a recent study from the University of British Columbia found that having a sugary "cheat" while on a strict keto regimen can actually damage blood vessels with an abrupt surge of glucose, following a long period of extremely restricted sugar and carbohydrate intake. Other observational research that exhibits associations with certain health outcomes points to long-term high-fat intake being associated with higher risk of stroke and heart failure. Moreover, some studies of children on a keto diet show high calcium levels in the blood, bone demineralization, and increased risk of kidney stones.

Despite the uncertainties about long-term safety, a keto diet clearly appears to have many immediate health advantages over the standard American diet. The question is: Are these advantages the result of achieving a state of ketosis by eating 75 percent of total calories from fat and only 5 percent from carbohydrates, or do they result from eating less sugar? Because, when you consume only 5 percent of your calories from carbohydrates, your diet will naturally be low in sugar. Sugar is found in carbohydrates, but not in fats or proteins. Transitioning from the standard American diet, with an average of seventy-one grams of sugar per day, to one that is extremely low in carbohydrates and sugar, should have significant benefits, regardless of whether the alternative diet is extremely high in fat or not.

Considering that reducing sugar intake has significant benefits, do we need to eat a high-fat diet to achieve ketosis in order to achieve weight loss and other benefits associated with a keto diet? And if we don't, are we risking our long-term health if we adopt a keto diet for a long period of time?

It is accepted science that micronutrients present in foods such as green vegetables and fruits are critical for overall wellness because they are packed with essential vitamins, minerals, and fiber. Many of these essential nutrients are difficult or impossible to obtain unless we eat these foods. Fortunately, some of the most nutrient-dense foods, such as kale, broccoli, Brussels sprouts, spinach, asparagus, cauliflower, tomato, blueberries, and raspberries, are extremely low-carbohydrate and low-sugar. That makes them important elements of any low-carbohydrate food plan. The standard ketogenic diet includes only a small quantity of these good vegetables and fruits, as it calls for no more than 5 percent of calories to come from carbohydrates.

Consuming more vegetables and fruits to take advantage of the essential vitamins, minerals, and fiber they contain will increase carbohydrate intake. And a diet that is more than 5 percent carbohydrates overall may prevent the body from remaining in ketosis. So, do we need to remain in ketosis in order to lose weight and realize the other benefits that result from a keto diet? The short answer is that you do not have to be in a state of ketosis to see results.

Ketosis is not the only way to lose weight and improve health. We can still achieve great results by following a nutrition plan that significantly reduces carbohydrate and sugar consumption when compared to the standard American diet, yet recommends eating more healthy vegetables and fruits when compared to the keto diet. The benefits of this alternative nutrition plan include obtaining additional vitamins, minerals, and fiber while reducing the unknown, long-term risks of a keto diet.

Aimee and Richard have written *Almost Keto* because they want to share with you an alternative way to eat. Their way is almost keto, but with a little bit less fat and a little more of the best carbohydrates, like vegetables and fruits. Their approach provides many of the same weight-loss and health benefits of a keto diet, while avoiding the unknown long-term risks of an extreme high-fat regimen. They offer a more sustainable way of eating that increases the variety of available foods and results in the consumption of more essential vitamins and minerals. *Almost Keto* provides a structured nutrition plan for you to follow that is similar to the popular and effective ketogenic diet, but allows for a fat, protein, and carbohydrate balance that is easier and more realistic to sustain, while yielding the significant weight loss and health benefits.

Introduction

W hen I was in my early twenties, my blood tests revealed I had high cholesterol. My LDL (bad cholesterol) was far higher than that of my peers, and I was gaining weight. My father also has bad cholesterol, so the argument that it was genetic made sense. I conceded to the fact that I would be on statin drugs by age forty, as advised by my doctor. With some doubt, I got my blood drawn and cholesterol tested by two other medical professionals by age twenty-eight and I was given the same verdict—genetically bad cholesterol that could not be changed even if I "became raw vegan." Essentially, I threw in the towel and decided that I would cross that bridge when I got to it, a decade or so later.

Flash forward to age thirty-eight. I had been to the doctor in the past decade but I hadn't specifically gotten tested or looked for results regarding my cholesterol—I was concerned and chose the "out of sight, out of mind" approach. At this point, my son was eighteen months old, so my husband urged me to get life insurance as a safety net for our family, if an accident or illness should unexpectedly occur. A nurse came to our house to conduct an extensive checkup with full blood panel and my results were received the following month. My husband was the one to open the decision and results from the insurance company, and his first words were, "Your cholesterol!" I turned away, saying, "I know, I don't need to hear—" "It's perfect," he interjected before I could finish.

Before "Keto" was a household name, I started the almost keto lifestyle back in 2008 when I was twenty-nine years old—a time when even though I was still relatively young, I had bad cholesterol and I was gaining weight, despite the fact that I followed most "healthy" mainstream American diet recommendations. I chalked my bad cholesterol luck up to genetics, because I ate the way most others ate, too, so of course, I determined that it was something that was out of my control, especially after hearing those words from three different medical professionals. I relayed my health and weight troubles to my then-boyfriend (and now husband and coauthor) and asked him what his secret was for maintaining a low body fat percentage and perfect blood test results, despite the fact that he is twenty years my senior. His answer (which I found quite counterintuitive at the time)—eat more fat.

The ketogenic diet that promotes weight loss from being in the state of ketosis, by consuming a large percentage of fat, is one of the most popular fad diets today. The diet's two primary pieces of criticism are that the requirement of 75 to 80 percent of calories coming from fat may be dangerous in the long term, and the sustainability of this restrictive food regimen is difficult for the average person to maintain. Almost keto incorporates healthier keto foods that are known to help with weight loss, inflammation, and overall wellness while consuming a moderate (as opposed to high) amount of fat. Different ways of adhering to the keto diet have been coined recently as many people are needing to find alternatives to the strict lifestyle. For example, "dirty keto" refers to the potentially dangerous approach of having carte blanche to all items such as bacon and bun-less fast food burgers. The term and title "almost keto" reflects the use of most keto-approved foods in a healthier and more sustainable manner, characterized by less fat and more nutrient-dense carbohydrates by way of green vegetables and low-sugar fruits.

Google trends charts have shown that the keto diet has been searched far more than the terms "paleo," "Whole30," and "intermittent fasting" in recent years. The popularity of the keto diet is on the rise, but there is conflicting research regarding the safety of consuming unlimited amounts of items such as bacon, cheese, fatty cuts of meats, and fried pork rinds. Aside from the safety concerns expressed by a variety of medical and nutrition professionals, quitting the keto lifestyle after a short-lived stint of weight loss is commonplace when dieters can't find sustainability in the food regimen. Another concern is the "keto flu," which is a term describing symptoms often experienced upon transition into the keto lifestyle—a characteristic of this "flu" is a variety of gastrointestinal issues, constipation being the most common. This rite of passage and supposed marker of progress is most likely a result from the lack of fiber and other essential micronutrients in the strict keto plan.

Generally speaking, many have success with weight loss and improved blood sugar levels when adhering to the keto food regimen, but should these results be attributed only to the fact that high levels of fat are being consumed? Coincidentally, keto foods are also low in sugar, and it has been proven, time and again, that consuming less sugar will result in weight loss as sugar turns into fat if not burned. Moreover, when one transitions from the standard American diet to a highly restrictive keto regimen, lower caloric intake will naturally ensue, also contributing to weight loss. Many keto dieters are coming to these realizations on their own but then seek guidance for their newly adjusted almost keto approach, as they do not have a formal plan to follow. *Almost Keto* provides you with a structured lower-fat, higher-fiber, higher-micronutrient nutrition plan while still employing cleaner keto-approved foods, allowing you to yield positive weight loss and blood sugar level results with a more sustainable and healthier lifestyle.

Chapter 1

Why Mainstream Dietary Recommendations Are Making Us Unhealthy

An estimated 160 million Americans are either overweight or obese. Of these 160 million people, almost 75 percent of American males and more than 60 percent of females fall into these overweight and obese categories. An added concern is that almost 30 percent of male and female adolescents under the age of twenty are also either overweight or obese—this figure has risen from 19 percent in 1980.[1] In addition, roughly 50 percent of all American adults have one or more chronic diseases, often related to poor nutrition. To put this in perspective, the most overweight country in North America is the United States with an obesity rate of 32 percent, compared to under four percent in Japan.

Roughly half the population in the United States is overweight or obese compared to ¼ the population being overweight in Japan. During a time of various medical breakthroughs and advancements, we must start questioning why our nation's health is on the decline. A driving factor of the dismal state of our well-being is the reality that after decades of adjustments and modifications to our dietary recommendations, we are still being told the wrong things to eat.

The USDA MyPlate has made some small improvements when compared to 1992's famous (and faulty) Food Pyramid, which suggested eating six to eleven servings of high-glycemic grains per day, as well as very little fat, despite how

---

1   Ng, Marie, Tom Fleming, Margaret Robinson, Blake Thomson, Nicholas Graetz, and Christopher Margano. "Global, Regional, and National Prevalence of Overweight and Obesity in Children and Adults during 1980–2013: A Systematic Analysis for the Global Burden of Disease Study 2013." *The Lancet.* May 28, 2014. Accessed February 06, 2019. https://www.thelancet.com/journals/lancet/article/PIIS0140-6736(14)60460-8/fulltext.

beneficial healthy fats are. However, many of the dietary guidelines for Americans still reek of monetary interests as opposed to the interests of the health of our public. Below is an example of daily food intake which meets the USDA MyPlate's dietary recommendations for a 2,000-calorie diet.

USDA MyPlate Daily Recommended Foods and Servings (2,000-calorie diet)

3 cups of nonfat or low-fat milk
2 pieces of bread
1 cup of cereal
1 cup of pasta
1 cup of orange juice
1 cup of sliced bananas
1 cup of sweet potatoes
1 cup of broccoli
½ cup of carrots
4 ounces of chicken
1 egg
1 tablespoon of peanut butter

One may look at these recommendations and nod at the fact that they seem "normal" for today's standards and, yes, they are normal; however, they are extremely faulty and actually contribute to serious medical conditions that run rampant in today's population, such as excessive weight gain and type 2 diabetes. Let's take this recommended daily intake of food and break it down into macronutrients (carbohydrates, protein, fat), as well as sugar so we can get a better understanding of the implications of these suggested foods. Take a look at the chart on the next page.

As you can see, this suggested example of one day of "healthy food" results in 108 grams of sugar, as well as an abundance of high-glycemic carbohydrates, many of which are coming from processed foods. This amount of sugar and carbohydrates is equivalent to eating almost eleven glazed donuts in one day! One may say that sugars from the above listed foods are different than refined sugar; unfortunately, your body is negatively affected by too much sugar, whether it is from a natural source or from a donut. Another possible argument is that these foods do offer a variety of nutritional benefits (unlike eleven glazed donuts), thus "justifying" the sugar and carbohydrate intake. We will explain in later chapters how to get twice the nutrients that this typical plan offers, while consuming less than half the

FOOD	CARBOHYDRATES	PROTEIN	FAT	SUGAR
Whole wheat bread (2 slices)	24g	8g	2g	4g
Whole-grain cereal (1 cup)	29g	3g	2g	7g
Whole wheat pasta (1 cup)	41g	7g	2g	2g
Baked sweet potato (1 cup)	41g	4g	0g	13g
Broccoli (1 cup)	9g	3g	0g	2g
Carrots (½ cup)	6g	0g	2g	2g
Sliced banana (1 cup)	34g	2g	0g	18g
Orange juice (1 cup)	26g	2g	0g	22g
Chicken (4 ounces)	0g	30g	4g	0g
1 egg	1g	6g	5g	0g
1 Tbsp. peanut butter	3g	4g	8g	2g
2% milk (3 cups)	36g	24g	15g	36g
TOTALS	250g	93g	40g	108 g

sugar, and no high-glycemic, processed carbohydrates (your carbs will come from healthier sources)!

Why is it so important that we reduce sugar and high-glycemic carbohydrate intake? According to the Centers for Disease Control, more than thirty million Americans (around 10 percent) are afflicted with diabetes and 90 to 95 percent of these people have type 2 diabetes, which is often caused by diets that include too much sugar. An added concern: type 2 diabetes is on the rise in groups where it used to be uncommon, such as children and adolescents.[2]

If you are unaware of how type 2 diabetes develops, your pancreas makes the hormone insulin, and insulin is the regulating component that lets blood sugar into the cells to be used for energy. In the presence of type 2 diabetes, the insulin cannot make the cells respond, which results in insulin resistance. The pancreas reacts by creating more insulin but will not be able to keep up, resulting in rising blood sugar, which then establishes an environment

---

2   "Type 2 Diabetes." Centers for Disease Control and Prevention. August 15, 2018. Accessed February 16, 2019. https://www.cdc.gov/diabetes/basics/type2.html.

for prediabetes and type 2 diabetes. Blood sugar levels that are too high are associated with a plethora of health issues including, but not limited to, excessive weight gain, heart disease, kidney disease, and vision loss. Fortunately, millions of these blood sugar-related ailments can be prevented or even managed with proper nutrition. Unfortunately, the current USDA nutrition recommendations that are provided to the public may actually cause these conditions—not prevent them!

You may be wondering, why are we told, by trusted governmental sources, to eat these foods if they may lead us down a path of type 2 diabetes, weight gain, and heart disease? The United States Department of Agriculture plays a heavy role in determining these recommendations and then these same guidelines are incorporated in the nutrition education curriculum which is taught to nutritionists, as well as some doctors. Essentially, as opposed to being based on scientific research and evidence, these recommendations are influenced by food producers, manufacturers, and special-interest groups. One of the USDA's largest priorities is to strengthen and support food, agriculture, and farming industries so these guidelines may be disproportionately based on profit opposed to the health of the general population.[3]

Every year, the food industry donates millions of dollars to politicians who are in charge of making decisions regarding food regulation. This results in the industry's ability to market foods that are laden with sugar, salt, calories, and unhealthy fats. For example, the United States Department of Health and Human Services, as well as the USDA, vetoed their own expert panel's suggestions to reduce processed meat and sugary beverage consumption in their 2015–2020 Dietary Guidelines, despite substantial evidence that those items are harmful to public health.[4] Through this orchestration of campaign funding and lobbying, the food industry has effectively squashed and avoided evidence-based guidelines and taxation. Therefore, the industry has been somewhat allowed to market, formulate, and sell foods that are proven to be detrimental to health when consumed in excess.

3   Nestle, M. "Food Lobbies, the Food Pyramid, and U.S. Nutrition Policy." NCBI. July 1, 1993. Accessed February 16, 2019. https://www.ncbi.nlm.nih.gov/pubmed/8375951.

4   Gostin, Lawrence O. 'Big Food' Is Making America Sick." NCBI. September 13, 2013. Accessed March 7, 2019. https://www.ncbi.nlm.nih.gov/pmc/articles/PMC5020160/

In addition to our own regulatory agencies, who should be protecting our health by providing accurate information regarding nutrition, we have product powerhouses such as Coca-Cola who have donated millions of dollars to researchers whose intentions are to downplay the effects of sugary beverages on weight gain. Of course we may expect this sort of underhanded activity when it comes to a large corporation that is trying to market its products, but we don't necessarily expect it from Harvard scientists. Back in the 1960s, Harvard scientists were paid by the sugar industry to minimize the link between heart disease and sugar. They had to name a new supposed culprit to take sugar's place and the scapegoat was fat.[5] Unfortunately this faulty, money-based science has been the foundation for a variety of nutrition guidelines throughout the past five decades and has led the masses down a path of falsehoods when considering sugar, carbohydrate, and fat intake in their daily nutrition regimens.

We decided to write *Almost Keto* because the current nutrition recommendations for the public are still based on old frameworks that were decided heavily by food industry lobbying. After seeing the advice that is offered through our governmental agencies, online, in several literary sources, and even in nutritionists' and doctors' offices, it's no wonder that millions of people are suffering from diet-related conditions despite the fact that they are, most likely, following mainstream nutrition advice. In these chapters you will find progressive and unbiased nutrition information that will be sure to put you on the right track for weight loss, toning, and impeccable health.

5   Damle, S. G. "Smart Sugar? The Sugar Conspiracy." NCBI. July 24, 2017. Accessed March 7, 2019. https://www.ncbi.nlm.nih.gov/pmc/articles/PMC5551319/.

Chapter 2

The Different Types of Keto, Explained

Odds are you have heard of the ketogenic diet before, but you may not be aware that there are several variations of the protocol. The general idea of the keto diet is to remain extremely low in carbohydrates while consuming an extremely high percentage of fat, so your body can be put into a metabolic state of ketosis. This state of ketosis causes your body to become efficient in burning fat (instead of carbohydrates) for energy. Before we explain the philosophy of almost keto and how it differs from the other current forms of keto, below is some keto background that explains six different popular keto regimens.

Standard Ketogenic Diet: Presumably the most popular form of keto, it typically calls for 75 percent fat, 20 percent protein, and only 5 percent carbohydrates. SKD is extremely low in carbohydrates (calling for less than fifty grams of carbohydrates per day), and is high in fat, while moderate in protein.

"Dirty" Keto Diet: One of the newer and fairly common keto trends, "dirty keto" follows the same macronutrient protocol (75 percent fat, 20 percent protein, and 5 percent carbohydrates) but it doesn't matter what foods those macros come from. Technically, one can eat unlimited amounts of bun-less fast food burgers, pork rinds, and bacon as long as those macros are in alignment.

"Lazy" Keto Diet: This version of keto doesn't call for tracking the amounts of protein and fat one consumes, but the "lazy keto" dieter does track carbohydrates with the intention of remaining as low as under twenty grams per day.

Cyclical Ketogenic Diet: This form of keto involves short periods of higher-carbohydrate intake, such as six standard ketogenic days followed by one high-carbohydrate day, also known as a "refeed" day. The refeed day consists of roughly 150 grams of carbohydrates.

Targeted Ketogenic Diet: Specifically for high-intensity athletes and body builders, this version of keto is very similar to the SKD, but focuses on adding in the daily allotted carbohydrates around workout times for added energy.

High-Protein Ketogenic Diet: Similar to the standard ketogenic diet, it includes a slightly lower amount of fat, with more protein, and the same amount of carbohydrates. The ratio is often 60 percent fat, 35 percent protein, and 5 percent carbohydrates.

As you can see, the most glaring common denominator among these six types of the ketogenic diets is the fact that the regular consumption of carbohydrates is extremely minimal, at 5 percent of the daily intake of calories, and the fat benchmark is much higher than typical recommended intake. So you can get a better idea of the implications of this type of food

regimen, let's break down a 2,000-calorie diet based on the standard ketogenic diet.

Total Calories	Fat Calories (75%)	Protein Calories (20%)	Carbohydrate Calories (5%)
2,000	1,500	400	100

Now to put this into perspective of grams of fat, protein, and carbohydrates to consume each day, based on the same 2,000 calorie/day diet, see the following table.

2000 Calories	Fat Grams/Day	Protein Grams/Day	Carbohydrate Grams/Day
Standard Keto Diet	167 grams	100 grams	25 grams

To achieve this breakdown of macronutrients in the standard ketogenic diet, on the next page is a sample one-day meal plan that includes SKD-approved foods. Keep in mind that the standard ketogenic diet allows regular consumption of some foods that many medical and nutrition professionals may deem unhealthy (for a multitude of reasons), such as bacon, pork rinds, hot dogs, deli meats, and low-carbohydrate fast food. Meanwhile, when following this same protocol, sticking to just 5 percent of your total caloric intake for carbohydrates doesn't leave much room to obtain vital micronutrient and fiber found in foods such as green vegetables and low-sugar fruits.

Standard Ketogenic Diet
Sample One-Day Meal Plan

Breakfast: 3 whole eggs scrambled, using avocado oil, and 3 pieces of bacon
Snack: ½ cup macadamia nuts
Lunch: Cheeseburger with no bun, topped with mayonnaise, 2 lettuce leaves, and 1 slice of tomato
Snack: 2 ounces (one small bag) of pork rinds
Dinner: 6 ounces of salmon, ½ cup sautéed spinach in coconut oil, ½ cup broccoli

Food	Calories	Fat	Protein	Carbohydrates	Sodium	Fiber	Sugar
Eggs (3 Whole)	234	15 g	18 g	2 g	186 mg	0 g	0 g
Avocado oil (1 tsp.)	40	4.5 g	0 g	0 g	0 mg	0 g	0 g
Bacon (3 Pieces)	129	10 g	9 g	0 g	411 mg	0 g	0 g
Macadamia nuts (¼ cup)	240	25 g	3 g	5 g	2 mg	3 g	0 g
70 percent lean ground beef (5 oz.)	465	40 g	20 g	0 g	95 mg	0 g	0 g
Cheddar cheese (1 slice)	113	9 g	7 g	0.5 g	174 mg	0 g	0 g
Mayonnaise (1 tbsp.)	94	10 g	0 g	0 g	88 mg	0 g	0 g
Romaine lettuce (1 large leaf)	5	0 g	0 g	1 g	2 mg	0.5 g	0 g
Tomato (2 slices)	8	0 g	0 g	2 g	1 mg	0 g	1 g
Pork rinds (2 oz.)	308	18 g	17 g	0 g	1030 mg	0 g	0 g
Salmon (6 oz.)	295	18 g	28 g	0 g	85 mg	0 g	0 g
Cooked spinach (½ cup)	23	0 g	3 g	4 g	0 mg	2.5 g	0 g
Coconut oil (1 tsp.)	117	14 g	0 g	0 g	0 mg	0 g	0 g
Broccoli (1 cup)	62	0 g	3 g	12 g	60 mg	5 g	1.5 g
Total	**2,133**	**163.5**	**108**	**24.5**	**2134**	**11 g**	**2.5 g**

Now that we can see what this standard ketogenic diet food regimen actually looks like on paper with corresponding macros, sodium, fiber, and sugar, there are different nuances of nutrition, weight loss, and overall well-being that should be explored when employing this type of nutrition plan. First of all, does this type of standard keto work for weight loss and blood sugar level improvement? Yes, studies have shown it to assist with weight loss and blood sugar level improvements, but the exact reasons as to why the keto diet can produce weight loss and blood sugar improvement results is still up for debate.[1]

One of the primary criticisms of the Standard Keto Diet is that the high intake of fats (good and bad) and low intake of carbohydrates is difficult to achieve in order to remain in ketosis. An added concern is that limiting carbohydrates such as green vegetables and low-sugar fruits will deprive one from obtaining critical vitamins, minerals, and fiber. Not to mention, consuming the foods that are needed to maintain at least 75 percent of total calories coming from fat isn't palatable for many and can be limiting, as well as time consuming. Many medical professionals question the long-term effects this dietary regimen has on various physical and biochemical parameters, as only short-term studies have been conducted.[2]

The reason why the standard keto diet (as well as the dirty keto diet) works is being attributed to the fact that one is consuming enough fat to be in the metabolic state of ketosis. But do you really have to be in ketosis in order to lose weight and improve blood sugar levels? There are other aspects of the keto diet (besides being in ketosis) that will promote weight loss and proper blood sugar levels, and we can still employ these same tactics for successful weight loss and blood sugar improvements without the unnecessarily high fat consumption. The four following tactics, which coincidentally are engaged in the standard keto diet, will contribute to substantial health and weight loss efforts.

1   Paoli, Antonio. "Ketogenic Diet for Obesity: Friend or Foe?" NCBI. February 01, 2014. Accessed March 23, 2019. https://www.ncbi.nlm.nih.gov/pmc/articles/PMC3945587/.

2   Dashti, Hussein, Thazhumpal Mathew, Talib Hussein, Sami Asfar, Abdulla Behbahani, Mousa Khoursheed, Hilal Al-Sayer, Yousef Bo-Abbas, and Naji Al-Zaid. "Long-term Effects of a Ketogenic Diet in Obese Patients." NCBI. September/October 2004. Accessed March 30, 2019. https://www.ncbi.nlm.nih.gov/pmc/articles/PMC2716748/.

AS A PHYSICAL THERAPIST, I see that patients often present to PT with idiopathic (of unknown cause) pain that is often associated with chronic illnesses such as obesity, arthritis, autoimmune diseases, or diabetes. Whether the patient is overweight or not, treating neuromusculoskeletal symptoms is insufficient without addressing lifestyle choices (e.g., diet, water intake, sleep, or stress management) and will not ultimately alleviate their pain in the long term without lifestyle changes. The standard American diet of foods containing a plethora of salt, sugar, and unhealthy fats while also lacking fresh fruits and vegetables directly contributes to inflammation and systemic pain.[3] According to the latest research, many experts believe refined sugar, processed meat, and unhealthy fats trigger an immune response to repair cellular damage, which is the body's response to injury caused by a poor diet. This diet-induced inflammation has the potential to cause joint pain, osteoarthritis, rheumatoid arthritis, and other chronic pain syndromes and degenerative diseases. These diseases cause a downward spiral of decreased health. People don't feel well, they don't exercise, they feel bad, so they treat themselves with foods for the mere sake of instant gratification and satisfaction. Oftentimes, a patient's pain can be significantly reduced by making diet modifications that lead to overall lower systemic inflammation levels.

According to Galland and colleagues (2010), markers of chronic inflammation are associated with major health issues such as osteoarthritis, diabetes, kidney disease, cognitive decline, recurrent miscarriage, and colon cancer. Diets that contain green vegetables and fruits have demonstrated anti-inflammatory effects compared to American diet patterns.[4] In addition, antioxidants, vitamins, minerals, healthy fats, and proteins have been shown to help heal injured tissues.[5] Furthermore, anti-inflammatory foods help reduce chronic inflammation and therefore inherently decrease pain and reduces progression of degenerative diseases.

In the case of arthritis and other inflammatory conditions, nutrition and physical activity should be included as a primary intervention. Recent research has corroborated the quote "Let food be thy medicine" in that appropriate nutritional interventions may be one of the most useful tools doctors have to improve overall health outcomes in their patients and specifically reduce inflammation.[6] People suffering from these chronic illnesses have the ability to change their lifestyle for the better by including proper nutrition and activity in their daily life.

—Jacqueline Cowan, PT, DPT

3   Towery, P., JS Guffey, C. Doerflein, K. Stroup, S. Saucedo, and J. Taylor. "Chronic Musculoskeletal Pain and Function Improve with a Plant-based Diet." NCBI. October 2018. Accessed May 23, 2019. https://www.ncbi.nlm.nih.gov/pubmed/30219471.

4   Galland, L. "Diet and Inflammation." NCBI. December 2010. Accessed May 23, 2019. https://www.ncbi.nlm.nih.gov/pubmed/21139128.

5   Percival, Mark. "Nutritional Support for Connective Tissue Repair and Wound Healing." *Clinical Nutrition Insights*, 1997, 1–4. Accessed May 23, 2019. https://acudoc.com/Injury Healing.PDF.

6   Tick, H. "Nutrition and Pain." NCBI. May 2015. Accessed May 23, 2019. https://www.ncbi.nlm.nih.gov/pubmed/25952067.

Consuming Less Sugar

Sugar consumption is the primary culprit of weight gain, type 2 diabetes, and a host of other ailments. The average American consumes seventy-one grams (or seventeen teaspoons) of sugar per day, which translates into fifty-seven pounds of added sugar per year, per person. When one shifts from the standard high-sugar American diet to one that is very low in sugar, weight loss and blood sugar improvements will naturally follow.

Consuming Fewer Carbohydrates

Like with sugar, when one adopts a dietary regimen that is substantially lower in carbohydrates, results will follow. The average person consumes 260 grams of carbohydrates per day, so when that number is cut exponentially, less sugar will be consumed as carbohydrates convert into sugar, and sugar turns into fat if not burned.

Consuming Fewer Calories

Consuming less sugar and carbohydrates will, of course, lead to lower calorie consumption. When we eliminate or limit "filler" foods such as sugary beverages with a meal, dessert following dinner, and empty-calorie main courses and side dishes, we will naturally consume fewer calories, and these calories will be more nutrient-dense, providing the fuel we need for a healthy lifestyle.

Eating Consciously

When a new dietary regimen is employed, we consciously choose to eat foods that are beneficial for weight loss and overall well-being, instead of maintaining the status quo of the standard American diet, and eating what we always ate before.

The four abovementioned characteristics that are proven weight-loss tactics happen to be the same traits found in the standard keto diet, and have nothing to do with the need for extremely high fat intake, or being in the state of ketosis. Of course, healthy fat consumption from particular sources is advantageous, so almost keto uses fat as a primary staple, but, it will be employed at more manageable levels and with intention to come from higher-quality sources. The following chapter, will show you how to utilize these same strategies with lower levels of superior fats, a larger variety of foods, more carbohydrates, and added micronutrients.

Chapter 3

The Almost Keto Four-Step Guide to Getting Started

Congratulations and welcome to your almost keto journey! When starting any new dietary regimen, there may be unanswered questions and even concerns, so this chapter will tell you everything you need to know to begin. In pages to come, we give you the four simple steps to take to become almost keto and see the results you have been looking for. Think of this chapter as your simple go-to guide so you can get started easily and quickly. In future chapters, we will go more in depth with detailed almost keto principles, niche keto foods you should know about, meal plans, and recipes.

Step ① Understand your macronutrients.

As we mentioned in the previous chapter, almost keto guidelines for fat, protein, and carbohydrates will be different than the standard keto protocol. The suggested

guideline (give or take) for your almost keto dietary intake is 45 percent fat, 30 percent protein, and 25 percent carbohydrates.

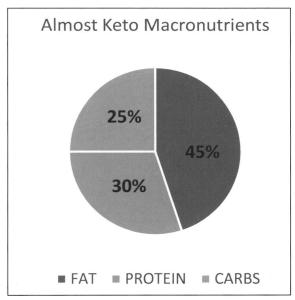

Almost Keto Macronutrients

45% — FAT
30% — PROTEIN
25% — CARBS

To be clear, to consume 45 percent fat in your diet, it means to get 45 percent of all of your calories from fat. For example, if you eat 2,000 calories per day, 900 of your total calories must come from fat sources. 30 percent of your calories will come from protein, so 600 calories will be from protein sources. 25 percent of your calories will come from carbohydrates since 500 calories is 25 percent of your 2,000 calories. To take the guesswork out, below is a table that shows how many grams of fat, protein, and carbohydrates you need from a variety of daily caloric intake requirements, starting with 1,200 per day and ending with 3,500 per day. Although the mainstream average number of calories to consume is 2,000/day, that number is wrong for many people, as required calories are determined by current weight, goal weight, gender, age, and activity level. Free calorie calculators can be accessed online so you can determine what is best for you and your goals.

Keep in mind, the following chart is a general guideline to give you an idea

Total Calories	Fat Calories	Grams of Fat	Protein Calories	Grams of Protein	Carbohydrate Calories	Grams of Carbohydrates	Daily Total
1200 calories	540 calories	60 grams	360 calories	90 grams	300 calories	75 grams	1200 Calories 60 grams of fat 90 grams of protein 75 grams of carbs
1500 calories	675 calories	75 grams	450 calories	112 grams	375 calories	94 grams	1500 Calories 75 grams of fat 112 grams of protein 94 grams of carbs
2000 calories	900 calories	100 grams	600 calories	150 grams	500 calories	125 grams	2000 Calories 100 grams of fat 150 grams of protein 125 grams of carbs
2500 calories	1125 calories	125 grams	750 calories	187 grams	625 calories	156 grams	2500 Calories 125 grams of fat 187 grams of protein 156 grams of carbs
3000 calories	1350 calories	150 grams	900 calories	225 grams	750 calories	187 grams	3000 Calories 150 grams of fat 225 grams of protein 187 grams of carbs
3500 calories	1575 calories	175 grams	1050 calories	262 grams	875 calories	219 grams	3500 calories 175 grams of fat 262 grams of protein 219 grams of carbs

*Calorie to gram conversions are based on nine calories per gram of fat, four calories per gram of protein, and four calories per gram of carbohydrate.

of the amounts of calories and macro-nutrients to consume to achieve certain weight goals. Does this mean you need to strictly adhere to calorie, fat, protein, and carbohydrate counting? Absolutely not! Sticking to the grocery list or the Perfect 10 foods in the following chapter, your macronutrients will naturally fall into place.

If you are already familiar with the keto lifestyle, you may be wondering if the above carbohydrate counts are for total carbohydrates or "net carbohydrates." The almost keto way of counting carbo-hydrates is simply going by total carbs on the nutrition label. Standard keto pro-tocols suggest subtracting grams of fiber and sugar alcohols from total carbohy-drates to obtain the figure of "net carbo-hydrates," but almost keto is already a bit higher in carbs and for ease of less calcu-lations, we will just go by regular carbohy-drate numbers.

Step ② Focus on higher quality fats.

As with standard keto, almost keto will still require you to focus on some fats, but they will not be as large of a proportion of your nutrition plan, as you are not aiming to "get into ketosis" to reach your goals. The most important difference between some forms of keto and almost keto is that we ask you to choose fats mindfully, opt-ing for the better versions and avoiding regular use of foods such as bacon, hot dogs, deli meats, pork rinds, and low-carb processed and fast foods. Aim to choose healthy fats that are monounsaturated such as extra-virgin olive oil, as well as polyunsaturated fats that have essential omega-3 fatty acids. Keep in mind, qual-ity is more important than quantity, so if forgoing an unhealthy fat (such as vege-table oil) means that you won't quite hit your 45 percent fat quota, that is perfectly fine. The next couple pages show snap-shots of some of our favorite fat recom-mendations, and you will find additional examples in the grocery list, as well as in chapter 4.

MIXED NUTS

PER 100 GRAMS
CALORIES   650

TOTAL FAT   58 g
CHOLESTEROL   0 mg
TOTAL CARBS   8 g
PROTEIN   19 g

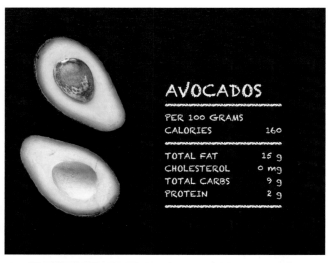

AVOCADOS

PER 100 GRAMS
CALORIES   160

TOTAL FAT   15 g
CHOLESTEROL   0 mg
TOTAL CARBS   9 g
PROTEIN   2 g

OLIVES

PER 100 GRAMS
CALORIES   115

TOTAL FAT   11 g
CHOLESTEROL   0 mg
TOTAL CARBS   6 g
PROTEIN   0,8 g

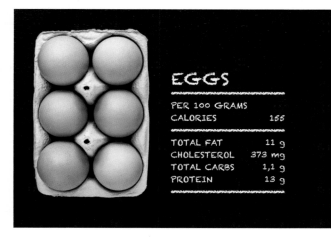

EGGS

PER 100 GRAMS
CALORIES   155

TOTAL FAT   11 g
CHOLESTEROL   373 mg
TOTAL CARBS   1,1 g
PROTEIN   13 g

Step ③ Get your grocery list.

Now that you know how many calories and grams of fat, protein, and carbohydrates you should be consuming, it's time to talk about food. The foods that will make up these almost keto percentages are keto-approved, meaning they are in alignment with all standard keto guidelines as they are low in carbohydrates and sugar, but they are mostly cleaner keto foods. Keto foods that may be considered "dirty" or have higher sugar and carbohydrate content (highlighted in orange) are advised to be consumed in limited amounts and are labeled as such in your grocery list. **The items highlighted in orange can be consumed in moderation** but due to a variety of issues including hormones in dairy, lower-quality fats, additives and preservatives, they are not for unlimited consumption. **All other foods highlighted in green can be eaten as much as you like** and in any combination to obtain your almost keto percentages of macronutrients of 45 percent fat, 30 percent protein, and 25 percent carbohydrates.

On page 18 you will find your Green Keto Foods list. The foods found in this category are the cleanest and most effective for your

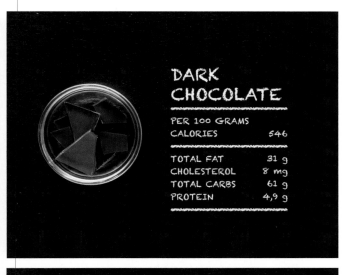

DARK CHOCOLATE

PER 100 GRAMS
CALORIES   546

TOTAL FAT   31 g
CHOLESTEROL   8 mg
TOTAL CARBS   61 g
PROTEIN   4,9 g

FULL-FAT YOGURT

PER 100 GRAMS
CALORIES   75

TOTAL FAT   3,8 g
CHOLESTEROL   13 mg
TOTAL CARBS   4,7 g
PROTEIN   5 g

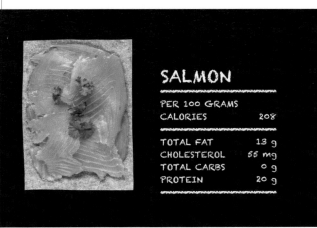

SALMON

PER 100 GRAMS
CALORIES   208

TOTAL FAT   13 g
CHOLESTEROL   55 mg
TOTAL CARBS   0 g
PROTEIN   20 g

almost keto regimen. You will see that some popular keto-approved foods are missing from this list, and you will find them on the following Orange Keto Foods list.

You probably noticed that some of the traditional keto staples are missing—items such as bacon, butter, cheese, and pork rinds. Though these items are high in fat and meet the macronutrient guidelines for the keto protocol, there are a variety of reasons (including but not limited to carcinogens, hormones found in dairy, excessive omega-6 fatty acids, as well as additives and preservatives) why the almost keto protocol does not endorse unlimited use of these products. The following Orange Keto Foods List includes many of these foods for your convenience, but we urge limited to moderate consumption at most. In addition, you will notice a few items found on the Orange List that are not part of the standard keto diet, as the almost keto regimen has a little more leniency for carbohydrate consumption. They do hold an optional place in the almost keto regimen for the sake of particular macro- and micronutrients, and for wider nutrition plan variety, especially for those who may adhere to a vegan or vegetarian lifestyle.

Fatty Foods and Condiments	Animal and Vegan Proteins	Low-Sugar Vegetables	Low-Sugar Fruits	Cooking Extras
Avocado	Amaranth	Artichoke hearts	Avocado	Almond milk
Avocado oil	Artichokes	Arugula	Bell pepper	Apple cider vinegar
Chia seeds	Asparagus	Asparagus	Blackberries	Avocado oil
Chicken (skin on)	Bison	Bok choy	Blueberries	Basil
Chicken thighs	Broccoli	Broccoli	Lemon	Black pepper
Coconut milk	Chia Seeds	Brussels sprouts	Lime	Cilantro
Coconut oil	Chicken breast	Cabbage	Olives	Cinnamon
Dark chocolate (at least 70 percent)	Clams	Cauliflower	Raspberries	Coconut aminos
Eggs	Cod	Celery	Strawberries	Coconut milk
Extra-virgin olive oil	Crab	Collard greens	Tomato	Coconut oil
Flaxseeds	Eggs	Eggplant ✗		Extra-virgin olive oil
Grass-fed/organic beef	Grass-fed/organic beef	Green beans		Flaxseed oil
Greek yogurt	Halibut	Kale ✗		Garlic
Herring	Hemp seeds	Kimchi ✓		Ginger
Krill oil (Supplement)	Lamb	Leeks		Nutritional yeast
Lamb	Mackerel	Mushrooms		Oregano
Macadamia nuts	Mussels	Peppers ✓		Paleo mayo
Macadamia oil	Natto	Pickles ✓		Parsley
Mackerel	Octopus	Radishes ✓		Rosemary
MCT oil	Oysters	Romaine lettuce ✓		Sage
Olives	Pork	Sauerkraut ✓		Sea salt
Oysters	Rockfish	Spinach		Soy aminos
Paleo mayo	Scallops			Tahini
Pecans	Shrimp			Tamari
Pine nuts	Sole			Tarragon
Pork chops	Spinach			Thyme
Pumpkin seeds	Spirulina			Turmeric
Seaweed	Squid			
Sunflower butter	Tempeh			
Sunflower seeds	Tuna (fresh or canned)			
Tahini	Turkey			
Tuna	Venison			
Walnuts	Walnuts			
Wild salmon (fresh or canned)	Wild salmon (fresh or canned)			
Wild salmon oil (Supplement)				

You may be wondering if you need to purchase all of the green list items in order to start your almost keto regimen, and the answer is no! The wide variety of foods found in the green list gives you flexibility with regard to your food lifestyle, possible allergies, and aversions. Feel free to pick and choose the green groceries you prefer the most. As mentioned previously, you are not required to count calories and macronutrients, as sticking to the almost keto green list, as well as the almost keto Perfect 10 foods (found in the following chapter) will help to ensure you are consuming proper amounts of fat, protein, and carbohydrates. If you would like a general idea of serving sizes, please refer to the chart below.

Fatty Foods	Animal and Vegan Proteins	Higher-Sugar Fruits and Vegetables
Almond butter	Almond butter	Apple
Bacon	Bacon	Apricot
Butter	Beans	Banana
Cashew butter	Deli meats	Cantaloupe
Cashews	Hard cheese	Carrots
Cheese	Lentils	Cherries
Chestnuts	Peanut butter	Grapefruit
Cottage cheese	Peas	Grapes
Cream	Pork rinds	Honeydew melon
Deli meats	Quinoa	Kiwi
Ghee		Nectarines
Peanut butter		Oranges
Pork rinds		Peaches
		Pears
		Pineapple
		Plums
		Pomegranate
		Soft cheese
		Watermelon
		Winter squash

Easy Serving Sizes

Serving of vegetables = a softball
Serving of fruit = a tennis ball
Serving of nuts or nut butter = a golf ball
Serving of green salad = a softball
Teaspoon of oil, butter, ghee, or cream = a thumb
Serving of meat, poultry, or seafood = 1½ to 2 decks of cards
Serving of cheese = 4 stacked dice
Serving of quinoa or legumes = a small fist
Serving of yogurt or cottage cheese = a small fist
Lunch Folate Total: 157 micrograms

Beverages

Now that you have your almost keto grocery list of foods, this area is dedicated to beverages. As boring as it sounds (but it's the truth), good old H_2O is your best bet when trying to shed the weight, tone up, and improve your health. We know plain water can get boring, so other beverage options include unsweetened coffee, unsweetened tea, plain sparkling mineral water, and homemade fruit-infused water (simply place your favorite chopped produce such as lemon, orange, cucumber, and mint in a pitcher of water and refrigerate). If you enjoy an occasional adult beverage, low-sugar selections such as red wine, white wine (non-sweet varietals such as chardonnay, pinot grigio, and sauvignon blanc), and vodka with soda water are almost keto–approved in moderation.

The Importance of Drinking Water

WATER, "GOOD OLD H$_2$O" is vital to all forms of life. Human bodies are made up of approximately 60 percent water, depending on sex, age, and body composition. Water is critically important to our bodily functions, yet due to busy schedules, many of us don't drink as much water as needed. We take in water through drinking as well as through the foods we eat. If we are physically active, pregnant, nursing, or if we live in a hot dry climate, drinking more water is necessary.

Water is important for a number of reasons including, but not limited to: regulating our internal body temperature, maintaining cognitive function, maintaining energy, helping with digestion, maintaining proper body weight, and lubricating the brain, spinal cord, and joints. Water also helps the body distribute essential nutrients and remove harmful chemicals.

Through perspiration and blood flow, water helps regulate our internal body temperature. Water molecules absorb and transfer heat very well. Our blood is primarily made of water, which has the ability to move heat away from the extremities toward our vital organs when we are exposed to cold temperatures, and it flows toward the skin's surface and releases excess heat during times of excessive warmth. Water also helps to expel excess heat through sweating because the water evaporates and cools the surface of the skin. Heat is also expelled through the lungs when we breathe. If we are dehydrated, we are less tolerant of temperature changes and can be more susceptible to problems like heat stress and heatstroke.

Water is also important for maintaining healthy cognitive function. Proper water consumption has been shown to improve concentration, memory, and mood.[1] Research shows that even mild dehydration, which is defined as 1–3 percent of body weight, can cause headaches, lead to fatigue, and impair concentration. Dehydration also is associated with anxiety and restlessness.

Our energy levels are influenced by hydration. Adenosine triphosphate (ATP), sometimes known as "the fuel of life," is an energy-carrying molecule that is generated in the cell mitochondria of all living organisms. The H$_2$O molecule is a critical component in releasing the energy contained within the ATP molecule, and this release of energy is important to our bodies because every task from healing an injury to exercising requires cellular energy.

Our central nervous system, the brain and spinal cord, needs water to act as a shock absorber. Drinking water has been shown to prevent migraines and reduce headaches.[2] Water

---

1   Pross, N., A. Demazieres, N. Girard, R Barnouin, F. Santoro, E. Chevillotte, A. Klein, and L. Le Bellego. "Influence of Progressive Fluid Restriction on Mood and Physiological Markers of Dehydration in Women." NCBI. January 28, 2013. Accessed May 23, 2019. https://www.ncbi.nlm.nih.gov/pubmed/22716932.

also helps to lubricate our joints. Proper hydration helps flush toxins out of the body, which can help to fight inflammation and keep joints healthy.

Water is important for digestion and weight loss. When we consume food, it moves through our digestive tract, from top end (mouth) to bottom end (rectum). Water allows ingested food to pass through our digestive tract more easily and smoothly. Dehydration is one of the most common causes of constipation. If your body is dehydrated, the colon, or large intestine, soaks up water from your food waste. This makes your stool hard and difficult to pass. Regarding weight loss, water also helps create a feeling of fullness, which prevents us from overeating. Sometimes when we think we are hungry, we are actually just thirsty.

Any healthy diet or lifestyle modification should include the addition of a daily hydration regimen. An easy rule of thumb is to aim to consume half your body weight in ounces each day. For example, a 200-pound man should aim to consume 100 ounces of water per day (about 12 cups). As previously discussed, our lives are increasingly busy and dependent on technology. There are a variety of tools to help busy people remember to drink water on a regular basis throughout the day. Many smartphones and watches have applications to help busy people remember to drink water throughout the day. Some people find it easy to count how many times they fill a water bottle or place colored rings on the side of reusable water bottle. Water is an essential component of our health and well-being.

—Jacqueline Cowan, PT, DPT

---

2   Blau, JN, CA Kell, and JM Sperling. "Water-deprivation Headache: A New Headache with Two Variants." NCBI. January 2004. Accessed May 23, 2019. https://www.ncbi.nlm.nih.gov/pubmed/14979888.

Step ④ Know what you shouldn't be eating.

Almost keto–approved foods help you lose weight and improve blood sugar levels because they are low in carbohydrates and low in sugar. With that said, any foods that are moderate to high in either carbohydrates or sugar should be eliminated or severely limited to see results. Some of the listed foods may be touted as "healthy" or "weight-loss-friendly" in some circles, but the sugar and carbohydrate content will negate your efforts.

This chapter has provided a snapshot of everything you need to know about getting started, but we will be going more in depth in following chapters; if you're curious as to why these abovementioned foods are not permitted in the almost keto lifestyle, please refer to chapter 6. In additional chapters to come, we will include more specifics regarding servings per day, food groups, nutrients, and meal plans, as well as over 100 almost keto recipes!

Bagels
Cake
Candy
Cereal
Commercial granola bars
Cookies
Crackers
Croissants
Donuts
Fast food and processed foods (even low-carb versions)
Fruit juice
Ice cream
Muffins
Other sugary beverages
Pita bread
Pita chips
Pizza crust
Potato chips
Potatoes
Rice
Soda
Tortillas
White or whole wheat bread
White or whole wheat flour
White or whole wheat pasta

Chapter 4

"Do's & Don'ts" of Almost Keto & the Perfect 10 Foods

The almost keto nutrition plan can be achieved by followings a simple list of "do's" and "don'ts," and stocking up on the "Perfect 10" will make following the guidelines that much easier. Since going almost keto is a bit different than standard keto, below we explain what to do and what not to do when choosing the best foods to eat for weight loss and wellness results. In the pages to follow, we will provide you with the "Perfect 10"—the ten best foods/food groups to have on hand to make sticking to do's and don'ts a natural process that won't require any guesswork on your end.

DO **concentrate on quality as opposed to quantity.**

It is imperative to keep portions and caloric intake in proper ranges, and a factor that is just as important (if not more) is making sure those calories are nutrient-dense. Eating 1800 calories of pizza, ice cream, and soda per day is extremely different than eating 1800 calories of green veggies, eggs, fish, low-sugar fruits, and nuts per day. Choosing foods low in nutrients is very dangerous and may lead to vitamin, mineral, and nutrient deficiency, which is linked to a host of health problems such as fatigue, osteoporosis, and even cancer. Moreover, when one eats a regular diet of empty calories and junk food, the body will have constant cravings as it's searching for the nutrients it needs. If you're one who prefers to track your calories and macros to ensure accuracy, that is perfectly fine, but you are not beholden to it if you stick to high-quality calories and consciously listen to your body when feeling satiated.

DO **focus on nutrient-dense, real foods as opposed to synthetic vitamins.**

Eating a diet of whole foods that provide the most substantial nutrient intake will eliminate the need to supplement with synthetic, hard-to-absorb commercial vitamins. Synthetic vitamins provide a false sense of security for many which can lead to consuming foods that are devoid of nutrition while relying on obtaining adequate nutrients from a supplement alone.

DO eat a considerable (but not excessive) amount of fats, but make sure they are healthy fats.

Almost keto urges against a "free-for-all" of consuming any and all fats just for the sake of fulfilling your macronutrient quotas. Most people do not consume enough omega-3 fatty acids because only certain foods contain them. Omega-3 fats are not produced by our bodies, so we need to get them from our diet; they assist with brain function, heart health, and reducing inflammation. Good fats also help our blood sugar levels remain even, and they can help us feel full for longer. Some examples of foods that have good fats are flaxseed, oysters, egg yolks, salmon, walnuts, mackerel, and avocado.

DO eat some carbohydrates but choose low-glycemic options.

Unlike standard keto, almost keto allows for more leniency when it comes to carbohydrate intake. The primary reason for this is because some of the most superior, nutrient-dense foods such as green vegetables and low-sugar fruits provide a variety of essential micronutrients, and your overall wellness is positively affected by a higher intake of those foods. If you're not aware of it, the glycemic index is a measurement tool used to gauge how carbohydrate-containing foods affect blood sugar levels. Low-glycemic carbohydrate choices such as green vegetables, berries, Greek yogurt, and some nuts help maintain even blood sugar levels and satiety by breaking down into glucose at a much slower rate. In addition, these low-glycemic carbohydrates are minimally processed and contain a variety of naturally occurring, bioavailable vitamins and fiber.

DO eat adequate amounts of quality proteins.

Just like with fats, we need to be particular when choosing our proteins, as some are much more high quality (and therefore, healthier) than others. If possible, organic, grass-fed, and wild varieties of poultry and eggs, red meats, and seafood are always your best option to help limit environmental toxins; also, these choices often have a superior composition of fats, with even more omega-3s. If organic, grass-fed, and wild assortments are not available, aim for non- and limited-processed whole cuts of poultry, meat, and fish such as chicken breast or legs, turkey breast, steak, fish, and regular eggs. These are far better selections than items such as hot dogs, deli meats, other packaged/processed selections with breading and other additives, and of course, fast food. For those who are vegan or vegetarian, tempeh, natto, seitan, and organic/non-GMO soy are almost keto–approved and moderate consumption of peas, beans, and lentils is okay, as long as you're sticking to your 25 percent carbohydrate guideline.

DO NOT consume high-glycemic carbohydrates such as bread, pasta, cereal, potatoes, and crackers.

People do need to consume carbohydrates to be healthy but what many don't realize is that carbohydrates are found in several foods—not just the obvious items such as bread, pasta, cereals, potatoes, and crackers. The not-so-obvious carbohydrates such as green vegetables and low-sugar fruits are consumed regularly, and they do add up quickly. Not eliminating or severely limiting your intake of the above-mentioned high-glycemic carbohydrates can create an abundance of unused carbohydrates, which will convert into sugar and then into fat. Not to mention, overconsumption of these foods cause spikes in blood sugar that can contribute to prediabetes and type 2 diabetes.

DO NOT eat or drink sugary foods.

The average American eats seventy-one grams of sugar per day—that's seventeen teaspoons! The recommended daily allowance of sugar is thirty grams for women and forty-five grams for men. Too much sugar is dangerous, because if you don't burn it, it can store as fat. Also, when products containing sugar (or products that convert to sugar) are consumed, the blood sugar rises, resulting in the need for the pancreas to release insulin. If you make your pancreas do too much work with regard to releasing large amounts of insulin throughout the day to control blood sugar levels, type 2 diabetes may result. Not to mention, the spikes in blood sugar and then the low that occurs soon after will cause constant cravings for food, so it's a vicious cycle!

DO NOT use "dirty keto" foods regularly. Even if a fast-food bun-less cheeseburger will help you achieve your macronutrient intake of fats, protein, and carbohydrates for the day, fast food and processed foods are not a part of the almost keto protocol. Yes, you may have heard from many people that a diet that consisted of regular consumption of these foods actually resulted in weight loss, but weight loss isn't the only goal of almost keto. Long-term health and wellness is just as important as weight loss—the two go hand in hand. While some may look to be an ideal weight from the outside, fast-food and processed-food consumption has been proven to cause issues on the inside, many of which go undetected before it's too late.

DO NOT shun green vegetables. When thinking of the keto diet in general terms, it has been stated time and again to severely limit carbohydrate intake even if the carbohydrates come from green vegetables because too many carbohydrates will kick one out of ketosis. Like we mentioned previously, we aren't concerned with being in ketosis, as the almost keto nutrition plan employs an extremely low-sugar strategy without the need for ketosis to see weight loss and blood sugar improvements. Green vegetables are ranked the highest on the ANDI (Aggregate Nutrient Density Index), which measures the amounts of micronutrients per calorie, meaning green veggies are extremely low in calories, while providing substantial amounts of vitamins and minerals. Although we provided a general guideline of 25 percent of your total caloric intake to be allocated to carbohydrates, by all means, if you're craving that extra serving of spinach, kale, or Brussels sprouts, go for it!

DO NOT take an "all or nothing" approach. Many popular diets require one to start over if a piece (or even a bite) of cake at a birthday party occurs. This train of thought can lead to reluctance, and even anxiety, when it comes to taking the first step to making a lifestyle change. There is misconception that proper nutrition has to be followed 100 percent of the time, and there is no wiggle room if you want to see results, but that can't be further from the truth. You will see progress (and lots of it) if you adhere to the almost keto principles and strategies most of the time, but not necessarily *all* of the time. There may be situations when a slip-up occurs or you even plan on a cheat meal for a special occasion—acknowledge it, don't feel guilty about it, and jump right back on the wagon.

Now that you have the "Do's and Don'ts" of almost keto, below you will find the "Perfect 10." These food categories are vital pillars of your almost keto nutrition foundation, and making an effort to incorporate as many of these as possible into your daily food plan will naturally result in adherence to the "Do's and Don'ts." If you are a vegetarian or a vegan, you will still find that over 70 percent of this list will be suitable for your nutrition lifestyle. Upcoming chapters will expand upon the "Perfect 10" and provide further assistance with structured meal plans, daily serving amounts, and recipes.

Green Vegetables

Nutrient-dense green vegetables should make up the majority of your 25 percent carbohydrate intake, and you can still eat several servings per day while remaining in this general parameter. Nutrient-dense vegetables are low-sugar, unprocessed carbohydrate sources, packed with micronutrients such as thiamine, riboflavin, folate, iron, magnesium, phosphorus, vitamin A, vitamin C, vitamin K, vitamin B6, vitamin C, calcium, potassium, and manganese; they are also chock-full of fiber, which will aid in digestion and regular bowel movements.

Avocado

Avocados have special properties as they are one of the only fatty fruits! Like nutrient-dense vegetables, avocados provide a variety of essential vitamins and minerals, as well as fiber. According to the American Heart Association, the monounsaturated fat found in avocados can help to reduce bad cholesterol levels and the risk of heart attack and stroke. An added benefit is that when one consumes fat, the brain gets a signal to switch off the appetite. Eating fat slows the breakdown of carbohydrates, which helps to keep sugar levels in the blood stable.

Eggs

Eggs are a nice mix of quality protein and omega-3 fatty acids. Some nutrition and medical circles advise to eat the egg white only, but we urge you to keep that yolk. It is popular belief that the yolk doesn't have any protein, but it does contain 2.7 grams, which is 45 percent of the entire egg's protein composition. The yolk also boasts the superior omega-3 fatty acids, vitamins A, D, E, B_{12}, and K, riboflavin, folate, and iron. Although eggs have been demonized in the past for containing cholesterol, numerous recent studies have cited a general consensus that cholesterol, primarily from egg yolks, poses very little risk for adverse effects on LDL (bad) cholesterol levels.[1]

---

1   Griffin, BA. "Eggs: Good or Bad?" NCBI. August 1, 2016. Accessed April 6, 2019. https://www.ncbi.nlm.nih.gov/pubmed/27126575.

Wild Fatty Fish

In addition to being a source of protein, fatty fish such as wild salmon (if you choose canned salmon, look for "wild Alaskan" on the label) contains omega-3 fatty acids as well. The omega-3 fats found in these types of salmon contain exceptional amounts of the vital DHA and EPA which are the long-chain omega-3s known for being most beneficial for eye, brain, and heart health.[2] In addition to their omega-3 fats, wild salmon contain high amounts of vitamin D, which can be difficult to find in most foods. Another fatty fish that you can get both fresh and canned, mackerel has even lower mercury levels and is at less risk of being overfished.

2   M. Singh, "Essential fatty acids, DHA and human brain.," NCBI, March 01, 2005, accessed September 5, 2017, https://www.ncbi.nlm.nih .gov/pubmed/15812120.

Low-Sugar Fruits

Low-sugar fruits such as tomato, bell pepper, blueberries, raspberries, strawberries, and blackberries are excellent sources of vitamin C! It is common misconception that one must drink orange juice (22 grams of sugar per cup) for vitamin C to protect the immune system from colds and flu. It is possible to obtain just as much vitamin C in whole fruits that have a fraction of the sugar. Also a great source of fiber, these low-sugar fruits provide a plethora of other micronutrients and phytonutrients that help to prevent disease and aid in your overall well-being.

Grass-fed, Organic Red Meat and Organic Poultry

Due to environmental toxins found in many animal proteins, it is ideal to consume organic and/or grass-fed selections whenever possible. When beef, lamb, and venison are grass-fed, the composition of the meat changes, reflecting an omega-3 fatty acid profile that is more similar to wild salmon. These essential fats contain docosahexaenoic acid (DHA) and eicosapentaenoic acid (EPA). DHA is critical for brain and eye health, as it accounts for 40 percent of the polyunsaturated fatty acids found in the brain, and 60 percent found in the retina. Both DHA and EPA are associated with heart and cellular health, as well as lower levels of inflammation. Poultry such as organic turkey and chicken provide B vitamins, iron, zinc, potassium, and phosphorus.

Nuts and Seeds

Vegan sources of protein, nuts and seeds are packed with nutrition, providing substantial amounts of good fats, complex carbohydrates, fiber, vitamins, and minerals. Aim to consume a variety of raw nuts and seeds to benefit from a broad spectrum of micronutrients. The nuts and seeds that will pack in the fat without a lot of carbohydrates are macadamia nuts, hazelnuts, Brazil nuts, pili nuts, pecans, walnuts, sunflower seeds, chia seeds, flaxseed, sesame seeds, pumpkin seeds, hemp seeds, and pine nuts. High in calories, a small handful as a snack or used as a topping on a salad will do!

Probiotic Foods

We all have "good" and "bad" bacteria in our bodies. Probiotics are known as the "friendly bacteria" and consist of *Lactobacillus acidophilus*, *Lactobacillus bulgarius*, *Lactobacillus reuteri*, *Streptococcus thermophiles*, *Saccharomyces boulardii*, *Bifidobacterium bifidum*, and *Bacillus subtilis*. Bad gut bacteria can increase for a variety of reasons (i.e., use of antibiotics, too much alcohol consumption, lack of physical movement, and smoking) so consumption of good bacteria via probiotics is beneficial. Foods that naturally contain probiotics are Greek yogurt, apple cider vinegar, dark chocolate, fermented soy such as tempeh and natto, and brine-cured olives. Known as a superior probiotic food, sauerkraut actually does not contain a substantially diverse amount of friendly bacteria; however, its organic acid content supports the growth of good bacteria.

Oils

Oils are a staple of the almost keto diet. However, not all oils are created equally, so choosing the highest-quality oils with the most beneficial fat profiles is imperative. In addition, the processing of some oils (such as the use of the neurotoxin hexane for extraction) can have detrimental effects on the quality of the oil, so that is another factor to consider. Some of the best oils for almost keto, based on fat content and cold-pressed processing, are avocado oil, extra-virgin olive oil, coconut oil, sesame oil, and walnut oil.

Water

Although it's not a food, water does get a spot on the "Perfect 10," as its importance is undeniable. One of the key staples of maintaining proper weight and health is to make good old H_2O your primary beverage, as it is sugar- and calorie-free. Water assists with dissolving vitamins and minerals, making them more accessible to the body. Also, adequate water intake is essential for the kidneys to function, which will assist with the excretion of waste products.

The Perfect 10 will lay a strong nutritional foundation for your almost keto nutrition plan and will provide much of the macro- and micronutrients you will need to achieve weight loss and well-being. You aren't required to stick solely to the foods found in the above ten categories, so feel free to refer back to your green and orange foods lists (found in chapter 3) for more variety. If you aren't familiar with some of the items listed thus far, the recipes found in chapters 17, 18, 19, and 20 will assist you with incorporating many of these foods into a variety of meals and snacks!

Chapter 5

Almost Keto Tactics for Success

Now that you're aware of the foods that will be employed during your almost keto journey, we would like to provide you with some additional tactics for success. Some of these address topics of food intake, while others talk about mental aspects of nutrition and weight loss. In addition, you will find pointers with regard to specific situations where sticking to a food regimen may be more difficult, and ways to overcome nutrition plan slip-ups (which happen to everyone)!

Tactic (1) Almost Everything Counts

Little decisions we make every day add up to create a significant long-term result. One may argue that a soda with lunch will not cause diabetes or significant weight gain, and that's correct; one soda will not do that. The problem is that one soda at lunch potentially turns into thirty sodas per month. Thirty sodas per month equal 278 teaspoons of pure sugar. Sugar turns into fat, once digested. Occasional splurges are realistic, but they have to be occasional and the portion size should be controlled. The "this one soda will not kill me" attitude may be detrimental if that train of thought is repeated over and over again.

If you maintain a consistently healthy diet, don't feel bad about splurging once in a while. A piece of cake at a birthday party is just fine—as long as you haven't had other servings of junk food that week. The most difficult aspect of this principle is being honest with yourself. If you feel as if you are not seeing results quickly enough, try jotting down all of your food and beverage intake for three days to see where some of the red flags may be occurring.

Tactic (2) Eat Consciously

Since counting calories and macronutrients isn't required in the almost keto lifestyle, a good rule of thumb to follow is to listen to your body and eat consciously. Eating consciously means eating when you are hungry and stopping when you are 80 percent full. It is easier said than done sometimes but when we eat consciously, we avoid eating out of boredom, stress, or social pressure. Also, it is best to provide focus on your food instead of allocating attention to a book or movie; many people tend to overeat while their minds are occupied by something else. If you prefer not to count your calories and macros, that is perfectly fine, but it can be useful to employ this "Seven Scales of Hunger" and try to always hover around level 4.

Seven Scales of Hunger

7. **About to burst:** Ate way too much food, but it was fun! Same feeling you may experience after Thanksgiving dinner or a birthday party and you think you may never want to see food again.
6. **Extremely full:** Feeling some discomfort/bloat and need to lie down.
5. **Pretty full:** Had a few extra bites after being satiated and won't need to eat again for some time.
4. **Comfortably satisfied:** Ate for fullness and not for sport; stopped when 80 percent content (this is easiest to attain when you eat slowly so your brain has time to signal to your stomach).
3. **A tad bit uncomfortable:** Didn't eat quite enough (around 70 percent full) and feel a snack (or more) is needed in the near future.
2. **Uncomfortable:** May have the "growling" sensation in the stomach and or experience low energy.
1. **Miserable:** Extremely low on energy, unable to focus on tasks, and possibly irritable.

Tactic ③ Control Calories and Portions

Like we have mentioned, counting calories is not required, but it can be beneficial to have a general idea of how many calories is right for you and your goals, since many people eat far more calories than their bodies need. Despite the fact that the main purpose of food is to fuel our bodies, it is commonly used for comfort, fun, social purposes, and a solution to boredom. Eating proper portions and not until you feel "stuffed" is a key component of achieving and maintaining your ideal weight. The average American is told to consume 2,000 calories per day, but this figure is completely wrong for millions of people. For example, if you are a woman who is 5'4 and want to weigh 125 pounds, your required intake will range anywhere from 1,400 to 1,800 calories per day depending on age and activity level.

Tactic (4) Stick to Your Grocery List

Before leaving for the grocery store, make a list and stick to it during your shopping trip. If you don't buy junk food and have it around the house, you are much less likely to eat junk food. For recommended grocery items, please see the green and orange food lists in chapter 3, as well as the "Perfect 10" in chapter 4.

Tactic (5) Eliminate or Limit Junk and Fast Food

Thousands of unhealthy, fattening, and dangerous food items have become "normal" and mainstream. A lot of these danger foods have become so socially acceptable that it can be thought of as strange to not participate in the consumption. It is critical to your weight management that these items be regarded as treats or special occasions—not typical, everyday food. Of course everyone is entitled to a splurge here and there, but it is imperative to severely limit servings of junk food items such as fast food, processed foods, pizza, soda, candy, cookies, cake, doughnuts, fried foods, and ice cream.

Tactic (6) Be Prepared at Work

The workplace is, typically, a junk food haven. Office donuts, cookies, chips, sodas, and candy vending machines are incredibly tempting, especially when you're hungry. Not to mention, unhealthy snacking may be common in your office, so the "everybody's doing it" attitude adds to the temptation of giving in. Not being hungry can be the most effective way of combating the weight-gaining food that's in your workplace. It only takes five minutes to put together a convenient snack pack that will keep your hunger satiated and blood sugar levels even. It's as easy as putting a few healthy snacks in a lunch bag in the fridge the night before work—items like hard-boiled eggs, raw nuts, vegetables and mashed avocado, Greek yogurt, berries, and healthy dinner leftovers.

Tactic (7) Healthy Restaurant Choices

You can still achieve your goals while dining out! If you have a hectic work schedule or you just enjoy eating in restaurants, try to employ the following key concepts when eating in restaurants. Of course, if you're going to your favorite restaurant for a special occasion, and you have stuck to your almost keto nutrition plan for the majority of the time, enjoy yourself!

- Skip the bread basket—even if it's put in front of you, kindly ask the server to take it away.
- Replace rice, potato, and pasta side dishes with vegetables.
- Use plain oil and vinegar for salad dressing.
- Eliminate pasta and bread-based dishes such as pizza, burgers, and sandwiches; if you order a sandwich or burger, ask your server to lettuce wrap it (most restaurants will oblige).
- Avoid soup—it's usually full of sodium, bad oils, thickeners, grain-based fillers, and other weight-gaining ingredients.
- Ask for any sauces on the side and try to use sparingly.
- Order fresh fruit or berries for dessert.

- Avoid waffles, French toast, pancakes, donuts, pastries, or hash browns at breakfast.
- If a restaurant meal is huge (and they usually are), take half of it home and have it for lunch the next day.
- National restaurant chains are required to have nutrition information on-site. Check it out—it may save you a thousand calories!

Tactic (8) Don't Drink Your Calories

A fruit juice with breakfast, Starbucks Frappuccino in the afternoon, and one soda at dinner add up to almost 900 calories and 100 grams of sugar! People can tend to ignore liquid calories and don't realize how easily they compile and result in weight gain. The habit of drinking water is a key staple to losing weight and achieving wellness. Unfortunately, soda and fruit juice have around the same amounts of calories, carbohydrates, and sugar. Even though fruit juice has natural sugar, it's still sugar, and sugar turns into fat if it isn't burned. If you're looking for a good source of vitamin C without the added sugar, opt for items like broccoli, bell pepper, Brussels sprouts, or raspberries.

Tactic ⑨ Step Off the Wagon—Don't Fall

If you maintain balanced nutrition on a regular basis, splurging occasionally will not hurt your weight-loss goals as long as you return to your good habits immediately after the splurge. Also, if you plan your splurges ahead of time, you will be nutritionally prepared to afford your treat. If you know you're going to a restaurant on Friday night that has your favorite chocolate torte, then be sure to stick to your nutrition plan on Monday, Tuesday, Wednesday, and Thursday and enjoy your night out on Friday. Once Saturday morning arrives, do not have the "I ruined everything last night so who cares what I eat today" attitude. Another key concept of weight loss is getting right back on the wagon after taking a controlled step off it.

Tactic ⑩ Avoid "Train Gain"

If you are one who enjoys exercise, avoid the big mistake of overeating—you will still gain weight, despite the fact you are working out. The average person's workout will only burn around 500 calories so it is imperative to stick to your nutrition regimen after an exercise session. Too many ice cream rewards for a job well done at the gym will backfire and negate all of the hard work you have put in.

We have all heard that people who work out need to "carb up" and eat more calories to have enough energy. This may be true for extremely competitive Ironman triathletes or Olympic athletes, but if you're working out like a typical person (jogging eight miles per week or spending 6 hours per week in the gym), there is no physical need to store away excess carbohydrates to be used for energy. Keep in mind, to lose one pound of weight per week, you must cut out 500 calories from your daily intake. If you spend an hour exercising, you can reach this 500-calorie deficit, and your work is done for the day. If you return home from the gym and reward yourself with four slices of pizza (1300 calories) instead of a sensible 600-calorie meal, you are now in excess of 800 calories. Not working out? Replace a morning scone with two eggs and some blueberries, and an afternoon soda with unsweetened iced tea, and there's your 500-calorie deficit!

Tactic ⑪ Don't Feel Obligated to Exercise to Make a Lifestyle Change

When it comes to weight loss and health improvements, you need to pick and choose your battles. For some, the thought of heading to the gym at 5:00 a.m. before a long day of work prevents many from ever attempting to make a healthy lifestyle change. Fortunately, weight loss and blood sugar improvements are primarily based on good nutrition—working out merely fine-tunes the effort one puts into their daily nutrition plan. If the thought of working out is holding you back from making a change, know that you are not required to exercise to achieve significant results.

Tactic (12) Keep it Simple

Nutrition can be complicated and overwhelming, but if you implement these seven pillars into your daily routine, weight loss and wellness will happen for you!

- Control portions
- Focus on nutrient-dense foods
- Eat healthy fats and high-quality proteins
- Use green vegetables and low-sugar fruits as a primary carbohydrate and fiber source
- Eliminate or severely limit high-glycemic carbohydrates
- Eliminate added sugars
- Exercise if possible (but it is not required)
- Make a plan, prepare, and stick to the guidelines.

Chapter 6

Foods to Eliminate or Limit and Why

As you have probably noticed, adhering to the almost keto lifestyle requires the elimination of some foods that are touted as "healthy" in some circles of the nutrition world, so you may be wondering why those particular items should be avoided. Also, if you're familiar with the standard keto diet, which allows unlimited consumption of certain high-fat, low-carbohydrate and low-sugar foods, you may be wondering why we are advising to limit some of those items as well. This chapter further explains the reasoning and philosophies behind the almost keto lifestyle through exploration of foods that should be avoided or limited for weight loss and overall health purposes.

Wheat Products

The majority of the health and nutrition world has concurred that white flour products are potentially weight-gaining, empty-calorie foods without much to offer in terms of vitamins and minerals. You may be wondering why whole wheat products are falling into this same category of foods to be eliminated, since they are generally thought of as a healthy requirement of one's diet. As we mentioned in chapter 1, according to the Centers for Disease Control, more than thirty million Americans (around 10 percent) are afflicted with diabetes, and 90 to 95 percent of these people have type 2 diabetes, which is often caused by diets that include too much sugar. In addition to obvious high-sugar sources such as candy and soda, foods such as whole wheat bread, pasta, cereals, and crackers contain many high-glycemic carbohydrates that will raise blood sugar when consumed. The drastic rise in blood sugar, resulting from regular consumption of these foods can lead to type 2 diabetes, cravings, and excessive weight gain. You may still be thinking this couldn't be true for whole wheat foods, as the composition of fiber

	White Bread	Wheat Bread
Serving Size	2 pieces (52 grams)	2 pieces (52 grams)
Calories	150	120
Fat	2 grams	1.5 grams
Carbohydrates	28 grams	24 grams
Protein	4 grams	6 grams
Sodium	180 milligrams	220 milligrams
Fiber	1.5 grams	3 grams
Most abundant ingredients per nutrition label	Enriched bleached flour (wheat flour, malted barley flour) water, high-fructose corn syrup	Whole wheat flour, water, high-fructose corn syrup, wheat, gluten, yeast

and carbohydrates is drastically different than that of white flour products, but that simply isn't true. Above is a comparison of whole wheat bread versus white bread. You will see they are extremely similar, the wheat having only marginally more fiber than the white bread.

Besides excessive high-glycemic carbohydrates, another implication of wheat products is that the majority of nonorganic wheat is treated with Monsanto's Roundup, which means that a large portion of processed wheat foods also contain glyphosate, a chemical found in the widely used weed killer. According to International Agency for Research on Cancer, glyphosate is classified as a "probable carcinogen." Several studies suggest consuming a "probable carcinogen" is detrimental to our health, and even the court system has recently ruled that it can cause unfavorable outcomes such as cancer. Keep in mind that most nonorganic wheat, as well as a multitude of processed foods such as cereals, pastas, and crackers that contain wheat have been treated with glyphosate—for more information about glyphosate and genetically modified organisms (GMOs), refer to chapter 15.

Coincidentally, the majority of foods that contain wheat are also highly processed with a variety of other detrimental ingredients. They have long shelf lives and contain harmful preservatives as well as other additives that will not contribute to your overall health and well-being. Some of these common ingredients that are found in processed wheat foods include but are not limited to soybean oil, high-fructose corn syrup, and soy lecithin.

The majority of US soybeans are, like nonorganic wheat, treated with Monsanto's glyphosate, therefore the widely popular soybean oil that is found in numerous processed foods is also contaminated with the "probable carcinogen." In addition, a high percentage of US corn is also treated with glyphosate, so not only does high-fructose corn syrup contain a "probable carcinogen," it is also even sweeter than sugar, and we know that excessive sweeteners can contribute to a multitude of health-related ailments. Soy lecithin is an additive that gives food a smooth texture; the chemical solvent, hexane (a neurotoxin) is used to extract oil from the soybeans, so traces of hexane will remain in these processed foods. In a nutshell, despite the fact that whole wheat products have been touted for decades as being required for a healthy lifestyle, there is a three-pronged negative with consumption of these products: high-glycemic carbohydrates, relatively low fiber-to-calorie ratio, and glyphosate/other toxins.

Cow's Milk

The marketing of cow's milk has been quite extensive, leading the masses to believe that it is a superior beverage due to its calcium content. Commercial cow's milk contains hormones that are meant for cows, not humans. Even the organic brands of milk contain hormones that are naturally found in the animal, and these estrogens and progesterone may not be ideal for human consumption.[1] In fact, some studies are suggesting that intake of commercial cow's milk may be cause of concern to the general public and more research may be needed.[2] Now if you like a little bit of creamer in your tea or a small serving of Greek yogurt (great sources of probiotics), that's one thing, but consistently high intake of dairy may be best to be avoided.

A rising concern is that pregnant cows continue to lactate, so they, too, are used in commercial milk production. The milk that comes from pregnant cows has considerably high levels of estrogen and

1 K. Mayurama, T. Oshima, and K. Ohyama, "Exposure to exogenous estrogen through intake of commercial milk produced from pregnant cows," NCBI, February 2010, accessed September 10, 2017, https://www.ncbi.nlm.nih.gov/pubmed/19496976.

2 H. Malekinejad and A. Rezabakhsh, "Hormones in Dairy Foods and Their Impact on Public Health—A Narrative Review Article," June 2015, accessed September 10, 2017, https://www.ncbi.nlm.nih.gov/pmc/articles/PMC4524299/.

progesterone, which are absorbed by one who drinks milk. This hormone absorption is linked with earlier sexual maturation in children as well as lowered levels of testosterone in males.[3] An added concern and irony is that many studies now show that milk consumption may be associated with higher incidence of bone fractures.[4] These are some alarming factors to take into consideration when pondering the common recommendation that you should be consuming three servings of dairy per day to meet your calcium requirements.

When following the almost keto protocol, keeping sugar intake to a strict minimum is essential to see results, and one cup of cow's milk contains thirteen grams of sugar, so following mainstream recommendations of three cups per day would result in thirty-nine grams of sugar just from milk consumption. So, what is one to do? Yes, we need calcium as it is an essential micronutrient especially for bone and heart health, nerve signaling, and muscle function. Fortunately, there are an array of superior nondairy sources of the nutrient, and we will tell you where to find them in coming chapters.

Starchy Foods

Like breads, pastas, and cereals, other starchy foods such as potatoes, bananas, and rice are not part of the almost keto nutrition plan due to high carbohydrate and moderate- to high-glycemic index rankings (which measures how carbohydrates affect your blood sugar). It's true—there are an abundance of micronutrients in the potato skin, but the white filling affects your body like table sugar does. In fact, in a recent long-term study of 120,000 individuals and the diet patterns that negatively impacted their weights, potatoes were identified as one of the primary culprits contributing to weight gain.[5] One medium potato has 37 grams of high-glycemic carbohydrates, which will create a surge in blood sugar, and, as we have

---

3   K. Maruyama, T. Oshima, and K. Ohyama, "Exposure to exogenous estrogen through intake of commercial milk produced from pregnant cows.," NCBI, February 2010, accessed September 20, 2017, https://www.ncbi.nlm.nih.gov/pubmed/19496976.

4   K. Michaëlsson et al., "Milk intake and risk of mortality and fractures in women and men: cohort studies.," NCBI, October 28, 2014, accessed September 20, 2017, https://www.ncbi.nlm.nih.gov/pubmed/25352269.

5   Mozaffarian, Dariush, Tao Hao, Eric Rimm, Walter Willett, and Frank Hu. "Changes in Diet and Lifestyle and Long-Term Weight Gain in Women and Men." *New England Journal of Medicine*. June 29, 2011. Accessed April 14, 2019. https://www.nejm.org/doi/full/10.1056/NEJMoa1014296.

mentioned previously, sugar will turn into fat if not burned. We don't want you to miss out on the essential nutrients such as fiber, potassium, vitamin B6, and magnesium that are found in the potato, so you can refer to chapter 8 to see which almost keto–approved foods boast those particular nutrients.

Rice is another starchy food that is commonly up for debate in nutrition circles. Just like white bread, white rice has been labeled as inferior, while brown rice is recommended for its higher fiber and lower carbohydrate content. Due to these characteristics of brown rice, it is commonly approved of as a weight- and blood sugar–friendly food. Below is a comparison of white and brown rice so we can examine the nutritional profiles of each to find any similarities and differences.

	White Rice	Brown Rice
Serving size	1 cup	1 cup
Calories	206	216
Fat	0.4 gram	1.8 grams
Carbohydrates	45 grams	45 grams
Protein	4 grams	5 grams
Fiber	0.6 gram	3.5 grams

As you can see, the only glaring difference is the fact that the cup of brown rice has roughly three more grams of fiber per cup than the white variety. This one characteristic has been the cause for many nutritionists and doctors to recommend brown rice as a healthy blood-sugar and weight-loss tool, as the fiber will slow down the digestion of the carbohydrates. The fiber content in the brown rice does make it a better choice, but what many studies do not identify is exactly how much better of a choice it is—some studies suggest that choosing brown rice is an improvement when compared to white rice, but only a marginal improvement at best. Forty-five grams of carbohydrates in one cup of any food is quite excessive, and those three grams of fiber are not going to substantially negate the effects that a food with this nutrition profile has on our blood sugar responses. In fact, some studies have suggested that substituting brown rice for white rice will have no positive effect on those who are at risk for type 2 diabetes.[6] Other studies have suggested that the nutrient profiles in brown rice, despite being superior to

---

6   Zhang, G., A. Pan, G. Zhong, Z. Yu, H. Wu, X. Chen, L. Tang, Y. Feng, H. Zhou, H. Li, B. Hong, WC Willett, VS Malik, D. Spiegelman, FB Hu, and X. Lin. "Substituting White Rice with Brown Rice for 16 Weeks Does Not Substantially Affect Metabolic Risk Factors in Middle-aged Chinese Men and Women with Diabetes or a High Risk for Diabetes." NCBI. September 01, 2011. Accessed April 14, 2019. https://www.ncbi.nlm.nih.gov/pubmed/21795429.

white rice, may have no impact on overall health due to low absorption rates, caused by antinutritional factors present in brown rice.[7] Just like with potatoes, brown rice boasts many essential vitamins and minerals such as fiber, vitamin B6, and magnesium. Chapter 8 will list a variety of foods that contain those nutrients, while having exponentially lesser amounts of carbohydrates, and therefore, more positive effects on your blood sugar and weight maintenance.

Sports Drinks and Fruit Juices

In addition to eating nutrient-dense foods, we recommend staying hydrated with water as your primary beverage. Water also includes unsweetened tea and coffee, as well as unsweetened sparkling water. We highly recommend against one of the most common beverage suggestions that many receive when trying to lose weight and/or improve overall health, and that faulty advice is to drink sports drinks for hydration and electrolyte replenishment.

CUTTING CARBOHYDRATES and calories are two great reasons to lower your rice intake, but here's another one: both brown and white rice have been found to contain inorganic arsenic, a highly toxic chemical that occurs naturally in water, soil, and rocks.[8] Arsenic levels have been on the rise in recent years due to pesticides, herbicides, coal burning, phosphate fertilizers, and various other sources. This can be especially concerning for people on gluten-free diets as many GF products are made from rice flour and other rice-based ingredients. While dietary arsenic does not typically cause immediate adverse health effects, it has been linked to several long-term illnesses, including cancer, heart disease, high blood pressure, and type 2 diabetes.[9] Because most of us don't have labs at home to help measure the arsenic content of our food and water, it seems advisable to either eliminate rice and rice products from your diet completely or eat them in moderation. Tips for removing arsenic from rice include thorough washing (this can reduce the amount by up to 28 percent), increased water when cooking, and using basmati or jasmine over other varieties.

—Katie Williams, RN

7   Callegaro, D., and J. Tirapegui. "[Comparison of the Nutritional Value between Brown Rice and White Rice]." NCBI. October/November 1996. Accessed April 14, 2019. https://www.ncbi.nlm.nih.gov/pubmed/9302338.
8   "Arsenic in Rice: Should You Be Concerned?" Healthline. Accessed May 21, 2019. https://www.healthline.com/nutrition/arsenic-in-rice#section2.
9   Arsenic and You Information on Arsenic in Food, Water & Other Sources. Accessed May 21, 2019. https://www.dartmouth.edu/~arsenicandyou/index.html.

Popular sports drinks contain a variety of sweeteners such as high-fructose corn syrup and liquefied table sugar that will not assist your wellness efforts. Even more alarming, some sports drinks contain harmful chemicals such as brominated vegetable oil. Brominated vegetable oil is a combination of bromine and vegetable oil and is similar in composition to brominated flame retardants; this additive used to remove any cloudiness to the appearance of the beverage. Banned in Japan and Europe, consumption of brominated vegetable oil is associated with thyroid disease, memory loss, fatigue, tremors, skin rashes, cancer, and hormone disorders.

Sports drinks are commonly suggested for electrolyte replacement, but the risks of consuming these sports drinks for electrolytes outweigh the benefits. Electrolytes are minerals such as calcium, potassium, sodium, and magnesium, and we do excrete them through bodily fluids, so, yes, it is important to replenish these minerals if you are an avid runner or gym goer. You can do so by eating mineral-containing foods including but not limited to vegetables, low-sugar fruits, fish, and meats.

You may be curious about fruit juices, given the fact that some mainstream advice suggests that sugar from fruit is natural and therefore, can be consumed quite freely, without consequence. Unfortunately, the sugar from fruit (fructose) impacts our blood sugar in a similar manner that table sugar does, therefore excessive sugar consumption from fruits and fruit juices is not almost keto–approved. Fruit juices are merely concentrated versions of the fruit itself, and you can see the sugar implications below when we take several pieces of fruit and condense them into one cup of juice. Not to mention, the commercial processing of juice strips the fiber content that is naturally found in the fruit. Below you will see the comparison of sugar and fiber found in one piece of fruit versus a cup of the corresponding fruit's juice.

	CALORIES	SUGAR	FIBER
1 orange	45	9 g	2.3 g
Orange juice (1 cup)	111	21 g	0.5 g
1 apple	78	15 g	3.6 g
Apple juice (1 cup)	113	24 g	0.5 g
½ large grapefruit	52	8 g	2 g
Grapefruit juice (1 cup)	96	18 g	0.2 g

Artificial Sweeteners

Artificial sweeteners add sweetness to foods without adding calories. Some keto circles approve the use of aspartame (Equal or NutraSweet), acesulfame-K (Sunett), and sucralose (Splenda) to give more flavor without impacting weight gain or blood sugar levels. Studies are now suggesting that regular consumption of artificial sweeteners by the general population is actually associated with negative health outcomes such as type 2 diabetes and metabolic disorders, as opposed to helping prevent them.[10] Not to mention, certain artificial sweeteners such as aspartame are associated with cancer risks due to carcinogenic properties.[11] Moderate use of stevia is approved in most keto circles as it is a zero-calorie sweetener that is derived from the plant species *Stevia rebaudiana*, native to Brazil and Paraguay. Although it is easier said than done, training your taste buds to not require you to add sweeteners to beverages and foods for satisfaction is a key staple of weight loss and overall health.

Processed Meats

Salami, bacon, hot dogs, sausage, and cold cuts fit into the protein and fat categories of traditional keto nutrition plans, so you may be wondering why you are finding them in this chapter of "what not to eat." We aren't saying you have to eliminate these foods altogether, but unlike standard keto and dirty keto, we do not advise eating several servings of these foods per week, despite the fact they do assist with meeting your macronutrient requirements. The primary reason we advise limiting consumption of these items is because they are very high in sodium and contain detrimental additives such as potentially carcinogenic nitrates, as well as butylated hydroxytoluene (BHT), and butylated hydroxyanisole (BHA), both of which increase shelf life (for a thorough examination of additives such as BHT and BHA, please refer to chapter 15). The regular consumption of additives found in processed meats has been associated with colorectal cancer, which is the first

---

10   S. Swithers, "Artificial sweeteners produce the counterintuitive effect of inducing metabolic derangements," NCBI, September 2013, accessed September 24, 2017, https://www.ncbi.nlm.nih.gov/pmc/articles/PMC3772345/.

11   Soffritti, M., M. Padovani, E. Tibalidi, L. Falcioni, F. Manservisi, and F. Belpoggi. "The Carcinogenic Effects of Aspartame: The Urgent Need for Regulatory Re-evaluation." NCBI. April 2014. Accessed April 14, 2019. https://www.ncbi.nlm.nih.gov/pubmed/24436139.

cause of cancer death of nonsmokers in affluent countries.[12]

Fast Food and Processed Foods

Fast-food meals are known to be loaded with empty calories, high-glycemic carbohydrates, sugar, and bad fats, but that is just the tip of the iceberg. If you order the typical burger, fries, and a soft drink at a fast-food establishment, you are likely to consume a combination of butylated hydroxyanisole, trans-fatty acids, dimethylpolysiloxane, and azodicarbonamide. If you have never heard of some of these ingredients and are unaware of their implications, you are not alone. These items are lurking in the majority of all fast-food items and have serious consequences for our health. As mentioned previously, for an in-depth examination of the abovementioned additives found in fast food and processed foods, please refer to chapter 15.

For your most successful almost keto journey, it is best to eliminate and/or limit the foods found in this chapter. We hope the explanations of the implications of these foods will provide knowledge that will, ultimately, help you understand why it may be best to avoid them. Fortunately, there is a broad selection of delicious whole foods to choose from when adopting the almost keto lifestyle, so keep reading on for a variety of meal plans and recipes!

12 Santarelli, RL, F. Pierre, and D. Corpet. "Processed Meat and Colorectal Cancer: A Review of Epidemiologic and Experimental Evidence." NCBI. March 25, 2008. Accessed April 14, 2019. https://www.ncbi.nlm.nih.gov/pmc/articles/PMC2661797/.

Chapter 7

Where Do My Almost Keto Nutrients Come From?

Going almost keto does not mean you'll be missing out on vital vitamins and minerals, as proper nutrients are plentiful when choosing the appropriate almost keto foods. Avoiding high-glycemic and high-starch carbohydrates such as bread, pasta, cereal, rice, and potatoes does not have to mean missing out on vitamins, minerals, and fiber, as there is an array of those nutrients in other foods, despite popular misconception that you need fortified processed foods to meet your micronutrient intake. You will find a variety of charts and tables in this upcoming chapter—we would like to provide a handy reference where you can quickly find the nutrients you're looking for, a general guideline of how much you should consume on a daily basis, as well as the corresponding foods that boast each nutrient.

Referring back to chapter 1 with regard to how our dietary recommendations are strongly influenced by lobbying, funding, and food manufacturers, when these types of vitamin and mineral charts are found on our governmental websites, the food source recommendations are comprised heavily of big-name processed foods that have fortified synthetic nutrients. Many of these foods consist of high-glycemic selections such as fortified juices, cereals, and breads, as well as other unhealthy foods such as margarine and vegetable oil. Once again, we must ponder these recommendations and question them being based on nutrition science and truth, as opposed to funding from special-interest groups. The following almost keto macro- and micronutrient charts contain unprocessed, whole foods that have naturally occurring vitamins and minerals.

Vitamins

Vitamin	Function	Food Source	Daily Amount
Biotin	Metabolizes protein, fat, carbohydrates for energy. Beneficial for skin, hair, and nail health.	Avocado, cauliflower, eggs, liver, pecans, pork, raspberries, salmon, sunflower seeds, walnuts	300 mcg
Folate	Metabolizes protein and assists with red blood cell formation. Prevents birth defects (pregnant women should consume 600–800 mcg per day)	Arugula, asparagus, avocado, beef liver, broccoli, Brussels sprouts, eggs, flaxseeds, kale, lemon, lime, walnuts	400 mcg
Niacin	Aids with nervous system functioning and digestion. Helps to convert food into energy.	Anchovies, avocado, chicken breast, ground beef, liver, mushrooms, peanut butter, pork, salmon, tuna, turkey	20 mg
Pantothenic Acid	Helps the functioning of the nervous system and formation of red blood cells. Metabolizes fat and aids in hormone production.	Avocados, broccoli, eggs, cauliflower, portobello mushrooms, poultry, salmon, sunflower seeds, yogurt	10 mg
Riboflavin	Assists with general growth and development, red blood cell formation, and energy conversion from foods.	Almonds, beef liver, eggs, lamb, mushrooms, oysters, poultry, spinach, tahini, wild salmon, yogurt	1.7 mg
Thiamin	Converts food to energy and assists with nervous system functioning.	Asparagus, Brussels sprouts, beef liver, nutritional yeast, macadamia nuts, pork, sunflower seeds, seaweed	1.5 mg
Vitamin A	Beneficial for vision, immune function, and reproduction. Assists with growth and development, as well as red blood cell, skin, and bone formation.	Broccoli, beef liver, butter, collard greens, eggs, goat cheese, kale, red peppers, romaine lettuce, salmon, spinach, trout	5,000 IU

Vitamin	Function	Food Source	Daily Amount
Vitamin B6	Assists with nervous system, immune function, and red blood cell formation. Helps to metabolize protein, fat, and carbohydrates.	Avocado, chicken, eggs, nutritional yeast, pork, ricotta cheese, salmon, tuna, turkey, spinach	2 mg
Vitamin B12	Helps to convert food into energy and assists with red blood cell formation and nervous system function.	Beef, clams, eggs, nutritional yeast, sardines, salmon, seaweed, trout, tuna, yogurt	6 mcg
Vitamin C	Assists with immune function and wound healing. Combats free radicals and helps with collagen and connective tissue formation.	Broccoli, Brussels sprouts, bell peppers, berries, lemon, lime, tomatoes	60 mg
Vitamin D	Regulates blood pressure and balances calcium. Promotes hormone production, bone growth, and immune and nervous system function.	Beef liver, egg yolks, herring, oysters, salmon, sardines, shrimp, tuna, responsible sun exposure	1,000–4,000 IU
Vitamin E	Strong antioxidant to combat free radicals. Supports immune function and blood vessel formation.	Almonds, avocado, Brazil nuts, broccoli, hazelnuts, peanut butter, pine nuts, rainbow trout, red sweet pepper, salmon, spinach, sunflower seeds	30 IU
Vitamin K	Supports strong bones and blood clotting.	Avocado, blackberries, blueberries, broccoli, Brussels sprouts, cabbage, cauliflower, collard greens, kale, mustard greens, spinach, Swiss chard, turnip greens	80 mcg

Minerals

Mineral	Function	Food Source	Daily Amount
Calcium	Supports nervous system and promotes bone and teeth formation. Assists with blood clotting, muscle contraction, and hormone secretion, as well as constriction and relaxation of blood vessels.	Almonds, broccoli, canned salmon, cheese, cottage cheese, fresh salmon, Greek yogurt, kale, sardines, sesame seeds, spinach, turnip greens	1,000 mg
Chloride	Converts food into energy and aids digestion and fluid balance. Promotes acid-base balance and nervous system function.	Celery, lettuce, olives, seaweed, sea salt, tomatoes	3,400 mg
Chromium	Promotes protein, fat, and carbohydrate metabolism and supports insulin function.	Basil, beef, broccoli, garlic, green beans, romaine lettuce, turkey	120 mcg
Copper	Promotes bone, collagen, and connective tissue formation. Assists with iron metabolism, energy production, and nervous system function. Antioxidant that combats free radicals.	Almonds, dark chocolate, kale, liver, lobster, oysters, sesame seeds, shiitake mushrooms, spinach, spirulina, Swiss chard	2 mg
Iodine	Supports thyroid hormone production, reproduction, and metabolism. Promotes general growth and development.	Cod, cottage cheese, eggs, Greek yogurt, green beans, kale, seaweed, shrimp, strawberries, tuna, turkey	150 mcg
Iron	Promotes growth and development, immune function, and energy production. Assists with red blood cell production, wound healing, as well as the reproduction system.	Beef, broccoli, clams, collard greens, dark chocolate, liver, mussels, oysters, pine nuts, pistachio nuts, pumpkin seeds, spinach, Swiss chard, turkey	18 mg
Magnesium	Assists with blood pressure and blood sugar regulation, as well as heart rhythm stabilization. Promotes immune function, bone formation, energy production, and hormone secretion. Strengthens nervous system function, muscle contraction, and protein formation.	Almonds, avocado, Brazil nuts, chia seeds, collard greens, dark chocolate, flaxseed, halibut, kale, mackerel, pumpkin seeds, salmon, spinach	400 mg

Mineral	Function	Food Source	Daily Amount
Manganese	Promotes cartilage and bone formation, as well as wound healing. Assists with cholesterol, carbohydrate, and protein metabolism.	Almonds, black tea, collard greens, green tea, kale, mussels, pecans, pine nuts, raspberries, spinach, strawberries	2 mg
Molybdenum	Promotes enzyme production.	Almonds, bell pepper, celery, cod cucumber, cheese, eggs, fennel, Greek yogurt, liver, tomatoes, romaine lettuce, sesame seeds, walnuts	75 mcg
Phosphorus	Promotes hormone activation, energy storage and production, and bone formation. Supports acid-base balance.	Brazil nuts, carp, cheese, chicken, clams, cottage cheese, liver, pine nuts, pistachio nuts, pollock, pork, pumpkin seeds, salmon, sardines, scallops, sunflower seeds, turkey, yogurt	1,000 mg
Potassium	Supports heart function, blood pressure regulation, fluid balance, and nervous system function. Promotes general growth and development, muscle contraction, protein formation, and carbohydrate metabolism.	Artichoke, avocado, broccoli, Brussels sprouts, butternut squash, clams, haddock, pumpkin seeds, salmon, spinach, sunflower seeds, Swiss chard, tomatoes, yogurt	3,500 mg
Selenium	Supports thyroid and immune function, as well as reproduction. Antioxidant that fights off free radicals.	Beef, Brazil nuts, chicken, clams, cottage cheese, crab, eggs, halibut, mushrooms, oysters, pork, salmon, sardines, shrimp, spinach, sunflower seeds, turkey, yogurt	70 mcg
Zinc	Promotes growth and development, protein formation, immune function, and wound healing. Supports nervous system function and reproduction, as well as taste and smell.	Almonds, beef, cheese, crab, eggs, green beans, hemp seeds, kale, pork, pumpkin seeds, lamb, mussels, oysters, pine nuts, sesame seeds, shrimp	15 mg

Now for a different perspective, on the next page you will find micronutrients categorized by food group and macronutrient categories. Just like the above vitamin and mineral sources, these following foods are also almost keto approved. If you're wondering how to incorporate these foods in a meal plan, you can refer to chapters 13 and 16, and for more extensive recipe ideas, please refer to chapters 17 through 20.

As you can see, the almost keto nutrition plan affords an abundance of all essential vitamins and minerals, despite the fact that many dietary recommendations suggest processed foods due to their synthetic nutrient composition. Some processed foods do, in fact, offer fortified vitamins and minerals; however, one can find several whole foods that offer naturally occurring nutrients with superior absorption rates. An added benefit is when consuming the abovementioned whole foods as opposed to fortified breads, cereals, pastas, and fruit juices, you will avoid high-glycemic carbohydrates that contribute to raised blood sugar levels and potential weight gain.

FOOD	MACRONUTRIENTS	MICRONUTRIENTS
Low-Glycemic Vegetables (broccoli, asparagus, Brussels sprouts, onion, cauliflower, spinach, kale, artichoke, collard greens, arugula, butter lettuce, romaine, Swiss chard, cabbage, radish, zucchini)	Carbohydrate	Vitamins A, C, E, and K; chromium, folate, fiber, pantothenic acid, vitamins B1, B2 and B6; manganese, selenium, pantothenic acid, niacin, potassium, phosphorus, choline, copper, omega-3 fatty acids, calcium, and iron.
Low-Sugar Fruits (blueberries, blackberries, raspberries, strawberries, tomato, bell pepper)	Carbohydrate	Vitamins A, C, E, and K, fiber, biotin, molybdenum, copper, potassium, riboflavin, thiamin, manganese, fiber, vitamins B2 and B6, folate, niacin, phosphorus, carotenoids.
Other Low-Sugar Fruits (avocado, olives)	Fat	Vitamins C, E, and K, fiber, copper, potassium, vitamin B6, folate, omega-3 fatty acids
Nuts and Seeds (almonds, pistachios, pecans, macadamia, Brazil nuts, pine nuts, walnuts, hazelnuts, sesame seeds, pumpkin seeds, chia seeds, flaxseed)	Fat and Protein	Vitamin E, vitamins B2 and B6, magnesium, zinc, fiber, biotin, copper, phosphorus, calcium, omega-3 fatty acids
Poultry (organic chicken, duck, turkey)	Protein	Vitamins B2, B3, B6 and B12; niacin, phosphorus, choline, iron, selenium, zinc, phosphorus, choline, and pantothenic acid.
Other Poultry (eggs)	Protein and Fat	Vitamins A, D, E, K; choline, vitamin B12, thiamin, riboflavin, folate, zinc, copper, and selenium
Fish (wild salmon, halibut, sole, rockfish, trout, tuna, anchovies, mahi mahi, opah, sardines)	Protein and Fat	Vitamin D, vitamins B5, B6, and B12, magnesium, potassium, niacin, phosphorus, and selenium; omega-3 fatty acids
Shellfish (oysters, clams, shrimp, mussels, crab, lobster)	Protein and Fat	Vitamin B12, iron, zinc, copper, omega-3 fatty acids
Meat (organic grass fed beef, organic grass fed lamb, venison, bison)	Protein and Fat	Vitamins B3, B6, and B12; omega-3 fatty acids, selenium, iron, zinc, phosphorus, choline, and pantothenic acid.
Dairy (Greek yogurt, cheese, cottage cheese)	Protein and Fat	Probiotics, calcium, potassium, vitamin A, vitamins B2, B6 and B12, zinc, phosphorus, selenium, and magnesium.

Chapter 8

Popular Nutrition Myths, Busted!

For decades, we have been told to eat particular foods in order to obtain certain vitamins, as well as to achieve specific health and wellness goals. Unfortunately, some of these foods that have been touted as superior sources of the nutrients we need are actually lower quality than what we have been led to believe by extensive marketing efforts. The myths we are about to go over stem from general blanket statements that have little to no credible statistics or research to back them up. Unfortunately, these myths—some of which are primary culprits in the deteriorating health of the general population—have spread throughout society as being legitimate and thus are followed by the masses.

Myth (1) You need whole wheat bread, pasta, and cereal to get your fiber!

The daily recommended fiber requirement is twenty-five grams for women and

FOOD	Calories consumed to reach 30 grams of fiber	Carbohydrates consumed to reach 30 grams of fiber	Sodium consumed to reach 30 grams of fiber
Whole wheat bread	1,350	270g	2025mg
Multi-grain cereal	1,275	275g	2300mg
Whole wheat pasta	1,260	246g	20mg
Avocado	702	36g	30mg
Flaxseed	550	30g	30mg
Strawberries	486	117g	6mg
Broccoli	465	90g	450mg
Kale	396	72g	300mg
Chia seeds	385	33g	13mg
Raspberries	240	56g	4mg
Artichoke hearts	195	45g	200mg

thirty-eight grams for men. Excellent marketing by the food industry has made people believe that whole wheat bread, whole wheat pasta, and whole-grain cereal are good sources of fiber. The truth of the matter is that you can get much more fiber per calorie in other sources of unprocesssed, natural foods. Below we compare different food sources of fiber and illustrate how much one must eat of a particular food to obtain thirty grams of fiber.

In addition to having more fiber per calorie, natural foods such as avocado, flaxseed, strawberries, broccoli, kale, chia seeds, raspberries, and artichokes are unprocessed and contain no artificial additives, but most commercial breads, pastas, and cereals do. Whole foods are superior when it comes to vitamins and minerals too. Breads and cereals are fortified with vitamins, which means they do not occur naturally, and, therefore, they are harder to absorb. The next time you are in a grocery store, look at the ingredient labels of breads, pastas, and cereals—you'll find a plethora of ingredients (such as sugar, high-fructose corn syrup, and preservatives) that are not ideal for weight loss, blood sugar, and overall wellness.

Myth ② Don't eat fish due to environmental toxins!

Yes, there are some fish to limit due to high mercury content such as tilefish, shark, and swordfish. However, many types of fish are extremely beneficial for macro- and micronutrient compositions. Wild salmon, for example is relatively low in mercury but high in protein and omega-3 fatty acids. As discussed previously, omega-3 fatty acids promote a variety of positive health outcomes, such as a lowered risk for heart disease, inflammation, arthritis, and Alzheimer's disease. According to the Natural Resources Defense Council, the following listed seafoods are the lowest in mercury.

Anchovies, Butterfish, Catfish, Clam, Crab (Domestic) , Crawfish/Crayfish, Croaker (Atlantic), Flounder, Haddock (Atlantic) , Hake, Herring, Mullet, Oyster, Perch (Ocean), Plaice, Pollock, Salmon (Canned), Salmon (Fresh), Sardine, Scallop, Shad(American), Shrimp, Sole (Pacific), Squid (Calamari), Trout (Freshwater), and Whitefish.

* You will see in following chapters that some almost keto meals and recipes incorporate canned tuna. If you are one who eats several servings of fish per week and are concerned about mercury intake, we recommend chunk-light tuna since it is three times lower in mercury than solid white albacore.

Myth ③ Drink lots of milk to get your calcium!

Once again, the marketing for milk has been genius—it does a body good, right? Or not so much. First of all, as mentioned earlier, cow's milk has hormones in it that help to grow very large cows! Even if you choose the organic brands, the hormones (intended for cows) still remain. Milk is touted for its calcium content and is known for building strong bones, but some studies suggest that calcium found in cow's milk has no correlation with strong bones and prevention of fractures.[1] Not to mention, at twelve grams of sugar per cup, it's not the ideal beverage for weight loss and blood sugar levels. For more beneficial sources of calcium, please refer to the table below.

Myth ④ Eggs will give you bad cholesterol and put you at risk for heart disease!

Despite eggs being a nutritious whole food, in 1968, the American Heart Association announced that all individuals should eat no more than three eggs per week due to their cholesterol content. Eggs also include invaluable vitamins and minerals, including vitamins B2, B5, B7, B12, and D, as well as omega-3 fats, high-quality protein, choline, iodine, selenium, and zinc. Because eggs contain cholesterol, they have been labeled as an unhealthy food that will contribute to raised LDL (bad) cholesterol and therefore, result in putting one at higher risk for heart disease. In 2015, the restriction of egg intake was

FOOD	SERVING	CALORIES	CALCIUM (mg)	SUGAR (g)
Sardines	3.5 ounces	210	351	0
Sesame Seeds	¼ cup	206	351	0
Collard Greens (cooked)	1 cup	49	300	1
Spinach (cooked)	1 cup	41	245	1
Canned Salmon	4 ounces	155	232	0
Fresh Wild Salmon	6 ounces	300	120	0
Kale (raw)	1 cup	33	101	0
Almonds	23 almonds	162	75	1
Broccoli	1 cup	31	74	1.5
Butternut Squash	1 cup	63	67	3

1   D. Feskanich et al., "Milk, dietary calcium, and bone fractures in women: a 12-year prospective study," NCBI, June 1997, accessed September 11, 2017, https://www.ncbi.nlm.nih.gov/pmc/articles/PMC1380936/.

eliminated from US dietary guidelines due to a lack of evidence that cholesterol from egg consumption actually causes heart disease. Many mainstream recommendations urge people to consume cereal or oatmeal for breakfast due to their being "heart healthy" despite the fact that those selections raise blood sugar (while eggs do not), but studies have shown that eating two eggs for breakfast in place of oatmeal reflects no change or increase in biomarkers related to heart disease.[2] In fact, more than fifty years of research has shown that the cholesterol in eggs has very little impact on LDL cholesterol levels, and is not associated with increased cardiovascular disease risk. Moreover, egg intake compensates for an array of common nutritional inadequacies, contributing to overall health and life span.[3]

Myth (5) You need fortified foods to get your folate!

Folate (otherwise known as B9) is famously known due to being imperative during pregnancy to prevent neural-tube defects, but folate is extremely important for the rest of the population too. Folate is required to produce red and white blood cells in the bone marrow, create DNA and RNA, and convert carbohydrates into energy. Synthetic folic acid (the manufactured form of natural folate) is added to a variety of processed foods such as breads, cereals, and pastas, and one of the primary reasons these blood-sugar-raising foods are touted as being healthy is because they contain fortified nutrients such as folic acid. Unfortunately, 40 percent of the population cannot metabolize synthetic folic acid, so consumption of these products may not help you meet your goal of required folic acid intake. There are, however, a large variety of low-carbohydrate whole foods that boast substantial amounts of naturally occurring folate that is far more bioavailable with higher absorption rates. See the next page for a chart of folate-rich foods.

---

2   Missimer, A., D. DiMarco, C. Andersen, A. Murillo, M. Vergara-Jiminez, and M. Fernandez. "Consuming Two Eggs per Day, as Compared to an Oatmeal Breakfast, Decreases Plasma Ghrelin While Maintaining the LDL/HDL Ratio." NCBI. February 01, 2017. Accessed April 27, 2019. https://www.ncbi.nlm.nih.gov/pmc/articles/PMC5331520/.

3   McNamara, Donald. "The Fifty Year Rehabilitation of the Egg." NCBI. October 2015. Accessed April 27, 2019. https://www.ncbi.nlm.nih.gov/pmc/articles/PMC4632449/.

Food Source	Serving Size	Folate Per Serving (mcg)
Cooked Asparagus	1 cup	262
Cooked Okra	1 cup	206
Cooked Spinach	1 cup	200
Cooked Collard Greens	1 cup	177
Turnip Greens	1 cup	170
Cooked Brussels sprouts	1 cup	160
Raw spinach	1 cup	110
Mustard greens	1 cup	103
Cooked broccoli	1 cup	100
Sunflower seeds	¼ cup	82
Strawberries	8 medium	80
Cooked cauliflower	1 cup	70
Romaine lettuce	1 cup	65
Avocado	½ cup	55
Flaxseed	2 tablespoons	54
Green beans	1 cup	42

Myth ⑥ You can get everything you need from vitamins!

Synthetic vitamin intake (as opposed to obtaining naturally occurring vitamins from food) has become a popular, quick fix among the general population. Store bought multivitamins are synthetic versions of real vitamins—they are made in a lab! Typical food intake and the standard American diet lack essential vitamins and nutrients, which creates the need for the ever-expanding market of fortified nutrients. If you eat a balanced diet of whole foods, you will get what you need for your health and wellness goals. Standard multivitamins are not easily absorbed and contain things like folic acid and ferrous sulfate—inferior versions of folate and iron that have low absorption rates, as well as side effects.

Myth ⑦ Stay away from fat!

It is true that many fats should be limited, but not all fats are created equally! We tend to overdose on omega-6 fats, which are found in items such as processed foods, vegetable oil, fast food, cookies, chips, and French fries, and then lack the omega-3 fats that are most beneficial for weight loss and heart health. Polyunsaturated omega-3 fats found in foods such as wild salmon, walnuts, flaxseed, seaweed, and grass-fed meats are not only beneficial for weight loss and lowered blood sugar levels, they are also associated with the lowering of blood pressure and risk for heart disease. Besides polyunsaturated fats, monounsaturated fats found in extra-virgin olive oil, avocado, and almonds also assist with weight loss, heart disease risk reduction, and inflammation.

Myth (8) You need several servings of whole wheat bread, pasta, and cereal to get your carbs!

Many nutrition resources recommend as much as 325 grams of carbohydrates per day, most of which come from gluten-containing foods such as whole wheat bread, pasta, and cereal. These types of carbohydrates are high-glycemic, which means they turn into a lot of sugar! Overconsumption of sugar is one of the primary causes of type 2 diabetes, and the sugar you don't burn off turns to fat, so it is critical to keep sugars and high-glycemic carbohydrates to a minimum. In all actuality, there is absolutely no real nutrition need for carbohydrate consumption to come from breads, pastas, cereals, and crackers, as low-glycemic options such as green vegetables, berries, and avocado, are unprocessed carbohydrate sources that have an abundance of naturally occurring nutrients and fiber.

Myth (9) You Need Fortified Milk, Juice, and Cereal for Vitamin D

Vitamin D intake is critical for bone and tooth health and support of the nervous and immune system; it also promotes lung and cardiovascular health, and may be associated with cancer prevention. Vitamin D is also one of the most common nutritional deficiencies due to the fact that it can be hard to find in foods. Below you will find a list of almost keto foods that have vitamin D; however, if you are one of the millions who are deficient in the vitamin, you may want to consider responsible sun exposure (around 10 to 15 minutes per day with no sunscreen) or consult with your doctor about supplementing.

Source of Vitamin D	International Units (IU) Per Serving
Fish Oil	1,000
Sockeye Salmon (3 ounces)	447
Canned Tuna (3 ounces)	154
Some brands of yogurt (6 ounces)	80
Sardines (two whole sardines)	46
Beef liver, cooked (3 ounces)*	42
Whole egg (1 large)	41
Swiss cheese (1 ounce)	6

You will receive a lot of advice (good and bad) when it comes to nutrition. Hopefully, we have cleared up some confusion for you by dispelling some of these popular myths. Nutrition can be complicated due to the never-ending and conflicting resources that are available in books and on the internet today. As previously mentioned, many aspects of nutrition science have come from studies funded by special-interest groups, so it is always best to scratch beneath the surface of some popular myths and recommendations and do your own research.

Chapter 9

Niche Keto Foods to Know About

There are several foods in the keto-genic world that are quite unique and possibly even unheard of in some parts. If you haven't heard of many of the niche keto foods or are unsure of what they are used for, you are not alone. The purpose of this chapter is to out-line and explain popular high-fat, low-carbohydrate, low-sugar items that may not be ones you, personally, have ever had in your grocery cart. The following list merely gives you more options that will help you achieve your almost keto macro-nutrient breakdown. If you are doing fine on your own with more mainstream foods, don't feel obligated to purchase or use any of the below foods. If you're looking for more options or you want to get more creative in the kitchen, you may find this chapter beneficial.

Avocado Oil Mayo

Regular mayonnaise can be used in your almost keto nutrition plan, but avocado oil mayo (or sometimes called "Paleo mayo") has a healthier fat composition due to the fact that avocado oil is superior to the oils used in standard commercial mayonnaise. Avocado oil mayo is higher in monounsaturated fats and extremely low in sugar and carbohydrates. It can be pricey in some grocery stores, but it is easy to make at home. It's a matter of combining avocado oil, eggs, lemon juice, and mustard; there are several recipe variations online. Avocado oil mayo can be used in tuna salad, for dipping roasted vegetables such as artichokes, or as a creamy base for salad dressing.

Bone Broth

Bone broth is made by simmering the bones and connective tissues of beef, pork, lamb, turkey, chicken, bison, venison, or fish. It is more nutrient-dense than standard broth and stock due to its longer cooking time, but the nutrient content is determined by the bones used in the broth. Animal bones are packed with calcium, magnesium, potassium, and phosphorus, whereas fish bones also contain iodine, which is important for metabolism and thyroid function. Connective tissue provides glucosamine and chondroitin, which support joint health, and marrow supplies vitamin A, vitamin K2, zinc, iron, boron, manganese, and selenium, as well as omega-3 fatty acids. The abovementioned components also contain the protein collagen, which turns into gelatin when cooked and produces numerous essential amino acids. As the ingredients simmer, the water absorbs the nutrients, so the vitamins and minerals can be consumed via drinking bone broth on its own or from its being incorporated in soups, sauces, and gravies.

Keto Coffee

Keto Coffee is a high-fat, high-calorie coffee that is typically made with brewed coffee, grass-fed butter or ghee, and MCT oil. It is suggested to use a blender to thoroughly combine the ingredients for a smooth and frothy texture. Since Keto Coffee does offer a substantial amount of fat and calories, some choose to use the coffee as a breakfast replacement. For a simple Keto Coffee recipe, see page 143.

Coconut Flour

Coconut flour is a naturally grain-free and gluten-free flour that is made from dried coconut meat. Coconut-milk production results in the by-product of coconut flour. High in protein and fiber, while remaining low in carbohydrates, coconut flour is popular in the keto and paleo communities for baking. For a coconut flour oatmeal recipe, please refer to chapter 17.

Coconut Oil

Extracted from the meat of mature coconuts, coconut oil is very popular in the keto community, as its fat profile is different from those of most other cooking oils. Typically, fats in the diet come from long-chain triglycerides, but the fats found in coconut oil are called medium-chain triglycerides (MCTs), as these fats are shorter, having between six and twelve carbons. There are four primary MCTs that are categorized, based on their carbon lengths— C6 (caproic acid) contains six carbons, C8 (caprylic acid) contains eight carbons, C10 (capric acid) contains 10 carbons, and C12 (lauric acid) contains twelve carbons. Because of their chemical structure, MCTs go to the liver, where they are used as a quick source of energy, and they can increase fat burning, as well as raise your HDL (good) cholesterol.[1] Coconut oil provides a mixture of all medium-chain triglycerides, and is most abundant in C12 (lauric acid). Once digested, lauric acid helps to create monolaurin, which helps to kill harmful bacteria, viruses, and fungi.[2] Coconut oil can be used for cooking at high heat, creamer for coffee, added nutrients in smoothies, and moisturizing the skin without added chemicals.

Dark Chocolate

Dark chocolate is an acceptable almost keto dessert or snack as it is high in fat while remaining low in sugar. Be sure to choose a minimum of 70 percent cocoa solids, as the higher the cocoa content, the lower the sugar. One glass of red wine has one to two grams of sugar so the pairing of dark chocolate with your favorite cabernet will make the perfect almost keto dessert.

1   Chinwong, S., D. Chinwong, and A. Mangklabruks. "Daily Consumption of Virgin Coconut Oil Increases High-Density Lipoprotein Cholesterol Levels in Healthy Volunteers: A Randomized Crossover Trial." NCBI. December 14, 2017. Accessed May 19, 2019. https://www.ncbi.nlm.nih.gov/pmc/articles/PMC5745680/.

2   Kabara, J., D. Swieczkowski, A. Conley, and J. Truant. "Fatty Acids and Derivatives as Antimicrobial Agents." NCBI. July 1972. Accessed May 19, 2019. https://www.ncbi.nlm.nih.gov/pmc/articles/PMC444260/.

Ghee

Ghee is clarified butter that is made from heating butter, which separates the liquid and milk portions from the fat. The milk turns into a solid, and the remaining oil is ghee. Since the milk separates from the oil, ghee is dairy-free and has a much higher smoke point than butter. Ghee can be melted over vegetables, used in Keto Coffee, or used in place of oil or butter when cooking dishes such as stir-fries or eggs.

MCT Oil

The primary difference between coconut oil and MCT oil is that coconut oil is comprised of around 55 percent medium-chain triglycerides, whereas MCT oil is 100 percent medium-chain triglycerides. In addition, while C12 (lauric acid) is beneficial to fend off harmful bacteria, viruses, and fungi, it is the most prevalent MCT found in coconut oil. Since it is the longest MCT, it is the least efficient in terms of converting to ketones. For greater ketone conversion, MCT oil contains a much higher proportion of of C8 (caprylic acid) and C10 (capric acid) which are known for brain health and curbing hunger. These specific MCTS will give you the benefits of a strict ketogenic nutrition plan, while being able to consume more carbohydrates. A 2015 meta-analysis found that MCTs helped to decrease weight, hip and waist circumference, visceral fat, and total body fat.[3] MCT oil has no taste or smell and can be taken on its own or added to coffee, smoothies, and salad dressings.

Nutritional Yeast

Nutritional yeast is a deactivated yeast with a cheesy flavor, found in flake or powder form. It is vegan-friendly and a substantial source of fiber, amino acids, and vitamin B12. Since it is very low in carbohydrates and sugar, it makes the perfect addition to the almost keto nutrition plan, especially if one adheres to a plant-based diet. It can be sprinkled on salads and entrées for added savory flavor, or made into a plant-based cheese sauce (see page 222 for the recipe), it makes a wonderful addition to most dishes.

---

3   Mumme, K., and W. Stonehouse. "Effects of Medium-chain Triglycerides on Weight Loss and Body Composition: A Meta-analysis of Randomized Controlled Trials." NCBI. February 2015. Accessed May 19, 2019. https://www.ncbi.nlm.nih.gov/pubmed/25636220.

Seaweed

Seaweed is a less commonly consumed vegetable, and it is one of the best vegan sources of omega-3 fatty acids. Seaweed and other marine algae actually have even more concentrated vitamins and minerals compared to vegetables that are grown on land. An excellent source of vitamin K, B vitamins, zinc, and iron, as well as antioxidants, seaweed can be eaten on its own, as a side dish, or in salads.

Shirataki Noodles

Shirataki are thin and translucent traditional Japanese noodles made from glucomannan, a fiber that comes from the root of the konjac plant. Shirataki are comprised of 97 percent water and 3 percent glucomannan; many studies suggest that glucomannan is associated with weight loss, as well as body fat and cholesterol reduction.[4] Besides noodles made from squash and zucchini, these are the only true pasta-like noodles that are acceptable in the keto and paleo communities as they are low in calories and carbohydrates, while still high in fiber.

Tahini

Tahini is a creamy nondairy butter that is made strictly from sesame seeds. In addition to being plant-based, tahini is high in healthy fats, moderate in protein and fiber, and low in carbohydrates. It's also packed with nutrients including copper, manganese, calcium, magnesium, iron, zinc, selenium, and thiamin. Tahini can be used in dips, sauces, smoothies, and salad dressing, or alone as a seed butter—please refer to page 175 for a creamy tahini dressing recipe.

We hope this chapter has been useful for you with regard to learning about foods that are often talked about in keto communities. Like we mentioned earlier, you don't need to incorporate these items in your nutrition plan; however, some can be very helpful for achieving your almost keto macronutrient combination. Not to mention, many find these additions to be unique and delicious, providing more variety in your grocery cart and meal plans.

---

4 Kaats, GR, D. Bagchi, and HG Preuss. "Konjac Glucomannan Dietary Supplementation Causes Significant Fat Loss in Compliant Overweight Adults." NCBI. October 22, 2015. Accessed May 20, 2019. https://www.ncbi.nlm.nih.gov /pubmed/26492494.

Chapter 10

Vegan Almost Keto:
A Plant-Based Option
by Joy Giannaros

This chapter is for everyone curious about including more whole, plant-based foods in their almost keto diet. A vegan (or plant-based) diet is abundant in fruits, vegetables, legumes, and other plant foods; it avoids all animal-derived foods such as dairy, meat, fish, and eggs. This chapter is the first of two chapters about vegan almost keto. This chapter illuminates that you can absolutely thrive on a plant-based diet, and the next chapter (Vegan Almost Keto: How-To Guide) shows how to succeed at eating high-fat, low-carb plant-based foods using the almost keto principles to achieve your wellness goals.

If you have recently become curious about veganism, you're not alone! The percentage increase of vegans in the last year has made veganism the largest-growing trend, resulting in *The Economist* dubbing 2019 as "the year of the vegan."[1] While we all know that veganism is popular among celebrities such as Beyoncé, Madonna, Ellen DeGeneres, Jennifer Lopez, Jared Leto, and Woody Harrelson, great thinkers such as Albert Einstein were vegan too. Even former US President Bill Clinton became vegan a few years ago, and giants such as Google are now paying attention and wanting to get involved. Entrepreneur Eric Schmitt (the founder of Google) predicts a plant-based revolution is coming, and named the consumption of plant-based proteins instead of meat as the number one "game-changing trend of the future."[2]

Fascinatingly, many athletes are becoming vegan and finding that their performance improves and muscle injury issues reduce. Football player Lionel Messi

---

1   https://worldin2019.economist.com/theyearofthevegan?utm_source=412&utm_medium=COM.

2   https://www.riseofthevegan.com/blog/google-confirms-the-plant-based-revolution-is-coming accessed May 2nd 2019.

(the best-paid active athlete in the world) was recommended to eat a plant-based diet by Dr. Guiliano Poser—a renowned sports nutritionist. "Vegetables, seasonal fruits and a good mineral water are essential fuels for our muscles. You have to reduce the intake of processed foods or foods contaminated with pesticides, herbicides, antibiotics, medications . . ." he says.[3] As a result Messi upped his goals per game by around 50 percent, increased the number of his assists, reduced his injuries, and improved his general play.[4] Olympic medalist heavyweight champion Barny du Plessis—the world's first vegan bodybuilder and Mr Universe 2014—also experiences major benefits. Barny claims that his meat-free diet has made him stronger than ever; he asserts that he now needs to train half as much on a vegan, GMO-free (genetically modified organisms), organic diet.[5] Other high-profile athletes are also finding a plant-based diet better for them, such as Venus Williams (who eats a raw vegan diet), NFL player David Carter, and Formula 1's five-time world champion Lewis Hamilton.

The benefits of a plant-based diet are not just anecdotal, however. Numerous studies and credible literature reviews, such as those by Dr. Fuhrman and Dr. Ferreri, have found that a vegan diet is a "healthful option for serious athletes. To maximize performance, recovery, endurance and resistance to illness, enhanced intake of beans, greens, seeds, nuts, whole grains, and other colorful plant products are recommended."[6] Recently in 2019, Neil Barnard, MD, FACC, and six colleagues found that "features of plant-based diets may present safety and performance advantages for endurance athletes." They explain that the performance advantages linked to plant-based diets include leaner body composition, effective glycogen storage, improved vascular flow and tissue

3   Brennan, Stuart. "Man City's Sergio Aguero Following Lionel Messi Diet Thanks to Martin Demichelis." *Manchester Evening News*, May 13, 2015. https://www.manchestereveningnews.co.uk/sport/football/football-news/man-citys-sergio-aguero-following-9239938.

4   Maylon, Ed. "How a New Diet Has Helped Lionel Messi Turn around His Season." *Mirror*, May 11, 2015. https://www.mirror.co.uk/sport/football/news/bayern-munich-vs-barcelona-how-5677591.

5   Kirkova, Deni. "Vegan Mr Universe, 40, Says Meat-Free Diet Has Made Him Stronger than Ever." Metro. Metro.co.uk, September 24, 2015. https://metro.co.uk/2015/09/24/vegan-bodybuilder-40-aims-for-mr-universe-title-as-he-says-meat-free-diet-has-made-him-stronger-than-ever-5351168/.

6   Fuhrman, J., and D.M. Ferreri. Fueling the vegetarian (vegan) athlete. *Curr. Sports Med. Rep.*, Vol. 9, No. 4, pp. 233Y241, 2010, page 238.

oxygenation, reduced oxidative stress, and reduced indicators of inflammation. Even though we may not all be athletes or aiming in that direction, it is interesting to see that plant-based diets are recommended and chosen by many who are relying on their physical performance for their livelihood.

While there are a number of reasons why people choose a plant-based diet, the biggest three are: better health, environmental factors, and ethical reasons. The primary reasons why you may be interested in finding out more about a plant-based diet is for your health, weight-loss, or wellness goals.

Health

The Academy of Nutrition and Dietetics in 2016 stated their position in favor of vegan diets: "vegan diets are healthful, nutritionally adequate, and may provide health benefits for the prevention and treatment of certain diseases."[7] The most comprehensive study of diet and death rates from cancer was described in Dr. Colin Campbell and his son Thomas Campbell's book *The China Study*. They discuss the monumental survey of diet and death rates from cancer in more than 2,400 Chinese counties and the enormous task undertaken to explore its significance for both China and America. This study resulted in strong recommendations for all to transition to a varied, whole, unrefined plant-based foods diet.[8]

Their recommendations do not solely apply to cancer, however, but link to all the main causes of death in the United States. In his book *How Not To Die*, Michael Greger, MD, coherently pulls studies together to assert that eating a whole-food, plant-based diet has been found to be capable of preventing, treating and even reversing every single one of the fifteen leading causes of death and other chronic diseases in the United States.[9] These include heart disease, stroke, cancer and even depression, as plant-based foods have been posited to positively affect people's brain chemistry, warding off depression, while components of certain other foods may

---

7   Melina, V.; Craig, W.; Levin, S. Position of the academy of nutrition and dietetics: Vegetarian diets. *J. Acad. Nutr. Diet.* 2016, Volume 116, Issue 12, pp. 1970–1980.

8   Campbell, T. Colin and Thomas M. Campbell. *The China Study*. Texas: BenBella Books, 2005.

9   Greger, Michael. *How Not to Die*. United Kingdom: Macmillan, 2016.

increase the risk of depression.[10] A large-scale, peer-reviewed study of over 65,000 people conducted by University College London showed that those who increased their servings of fruits and vegetables to seven a day reduced their risk of premature death by 42 percent.[11] Therefore, you don't even have to be fully vegan to tap in to some of the benefits. Simply increasing our servings of fruits and vegetables can have wonderful benefits for our health and well-being.

Weight loss

Whole-food, plant-based diets are perfect for people who just love to eat! Fruits and vegetables are made up of 80 to 90 percent of water on average, meaning you can actually eat *more* food but gain less weight. Experiments have shown that people tend to eat the same amount of food at a meal, regardless of calorie count. This is thought to be because "stretch receptors in the stomach send signals to the brain after a certain volume of food has been ingested."[12] Even if various plates of food contain 100 calories, the volume can be vastly different, which is why it makes sense that 100 calories of the plant-based foods are more likely to fill you up. What this means is that you can have an overflowing popcorn-bowl-sized serving of whole, plant foods during your meals and lose weight without ever feeling hungry. It's no wonder that many claim to have lost weight on a plant-based diet, including Bill Clinton, who shed a whopping twenty-four pounds by eating in this way.[13]

Whether it is because of the volume you can eat on a plant-based diet or not, credible studies show that a vegan diet can be a very effective way, if not the most effective way, to lose weight. A major study published in the *Journal of General Internal Medicine* reviewed twelve diet trials and found that people on a vegan diet lost the most weight.[14] Interestingly,

---

10 Greger, Michael. *How Not to Die*. United Kingdom: Macmillan, 2016, p 281.

11 Oyebode O, Gordon-Dseagu V, Walker A, et al. Fruit and vegetable consumption and all-cause, cancer and CVD mortality: analysis of Health Survey for England data. *J Epidemiol Community Health* 2014;68:856–862.

12 Michael Greger, MD. *How Not to Die* (UK: Macmillan, 2016), 110.

13 http://holisticholidayatsea.com/the-bill-clinton-vegan-diet/ accessed 5th May.

14 Huang, RY., Huang, CC., Hu, F.B. et al. Vegetarian Diets and Weight Reduction: a Meta-Analysis of Randomized Controlled Trials, *Journal of General Internal Medicine*, 2016; vol 31, issue 1: pg 109—116. https://doi.org/10.1007/s11606-015-3390-7, accessed 5th May 2019.

the largest study ever to compare the obesity rates of meat eaters, flexitarians, pesco-vegetarians, vegetarians, and vegans discovered that the only dietary group to be of ideal weight were the vegans, whose BMI averaged 23.6.[15]

Common concerns and myths

But what about protein, iron, calcium, omega-3 and B12? Is it really possible to get everything we need from a vegan diet? The answer is absolutely! It can be hard to imagine this is possible, as most of us have been brought up with deep-rooted food and nutrition links such as "drink milk to get your calcium," "eat red meat to get your iron," and "fish for omega-3," etc. However, as we mention in the first chapter of this book, the nutrition recommendations for the public are still based on old frameworks that were decided heavily on through food-industry lobbying. The dairy and meat industry have heavily influenced nutrition recommendations because the more people buy their products, the more profit they will make.

Isn't it surprising that despite processed meat being classified by the World Health Organization and the International Agency for Research on Cancer as having the highest carcinogenic level alongside asbestos and tobacco,[16] very few of us know about this danger? While many cigarette packets show disturbing images of what can happen to our bodies with tobacco use, there are no health warnings on packets of bacon or sausages or canned meat. Some writers believe this in part to be because of a direct conflict between federal protection of the rights of food lobbyists to act in their own self-interest, and federal responsibility to promote the nutritional health of the public.[17] Marion Nestle, in her report published in the *International Journal of Health Services* states:

> Since 1977 […] under pressure from meat producers, federal dietary advice has evolved from "decrease consumption of meat" to "have two or three (daily) servings." Thus,

---

15   Tonstad S, Butler T, Yan R, Fraser GE. Type of vegetarian diet, body weight, and prevalence of type 2 diabetes. *Diabetes Care*. 2009;32(5);791-6.

16   https://monographs.iarc.fr/list_of_classifications/ List of Cancer classifications. Accessed 8th May 2019.

17   Marion Nestle, Food Lobbies, the Food Pyramid, and U.S. Nutrition Policy, *International Journal of Health Services*, First Published July 1, 1993 at http://journals.sagepub.com/doi/10.2190/32F2-2PFB-MEG7-8HPU.

this recent incident also highlights the inherent conflict of interest in the Department of Agriculture's dual mandates to promote US agricultural products and to advise the public about healthy food choices.[18]

Therefore, the nutrition advice we are given is heavily influenced by food lobbyists whose primary concern is their own profit.[19] Indeed, there is little profit motive in our good health. Consequently, we need to look past the deep-rooted food and nutrition connections we are surrounded with, and analyze the evidence for ourselves. So, let's focus on some of the main concerns: protein, iron, calcium, and omega-3.

Protein

Protein is a macronutrient that helps build, maintain, and repair body tissue. Protein is composed of long chains of amino acids which, when we ingest them, are deconstructed and then built back together in order to be used in the body. Protein

amino acids are made by plants; animals do not make protein, instead, they get it by eating plants. Indeed, rhinos, elephants, gorillas, and horses, which are considered to be some of the strongest animals in the world, all get their protein from plants. The question is therefore whether *humans* need to consume animal meat for protein or whether we can get it directly from the plants themselves.

Biologically, humans are herbivores, meaning that we are capable of getting all the nutrition we need from plants. For example, we have hands, not claws; we have flat teeth that chew sideways rather than up and down, as is needed to tear flesh, and we have incredibly long intestines to give us time to extract the nutrients we need from plant foods. Carnivorous animals have short intestines so that the raw meat they consume can exit quickly before it rots inside their bodies. Furthermore, humans generally cook their animal protein; this can denature the amino acids and make them largely unavailable for our body's

---

18 Marion Nestle, *International Journal of Health Services*, First Published July 1, 1993 at http://journals.sagepub.com /doi/10.2190/32F2-2PFB-MEG7-8HPU.

19 (For a good collection of articles, reports and links on The Influence of Meat & Dairy Industry on Government, Education, News, Media & Health Professionals see website https://eatingourfuture.wordpress.com/meat-dairy-industry-influences-politics-government-education-news-media/).

use.[20] Indeed, The Max Planck Institute for Nutritional Research in Germany discovered that cooking destroys about 50 percent of the bioavailability of protein for humans.[21] Vegetables, on the other hand, are packed with easily assimilated amino acids and therefore less energy is needed to digest them. In this way plant protein is often thought of as a superior protein for humans to consume.

The protein debate, however, does not often discuss this. Instead, it tends to center around discussing the importance of consuming the eight essential amino acids we need from our diet alone, and eating "complete" proteins. Animal meat is said to contain complete proteins because it contains all the eight essential amino acids in amounts that meet or exceed human requirements. Plant foods such as fruits, vegetables, seeds, sprouts, and nuts also contain the eight essential amino acids in abundance, and foods such as soy and quinoa are considered complete proteins.[22] In all actuality, we do not need to be concerned with consuming "complete" proteins in each meal, as it is simply not necessary. The American Dietetic Association in 1993 concluded that the practice of combining complementary proteins is unnecessary, as research indicated that an assortment of plant foods eaten over the course of a day can provide all essential amino acids.[23] This is because the body can store amino acids to form complete proteins throughout the course of the day.

It is, therefore, clear that plants can provide us with all the protein we require, in case the vegan lifestyle is one that you currently follow or are interested in following. Indeed, we need to look no further

20 Snyder, Kimberly. *The Beauty Detox Solution*. Harlequin Enterprises (Australia) Pty, Limited, 2011.

21 Cousens, Gabriel. *Rainbow Green Live-Food Cuisine*. Berkeley, CA: North Atlantic Books, 2003, p. 56.

22 M. Messina and V. Messina, "The role of soy in vegetarian diets," *Nutrients*, 2(8), August 2010, 855–888. doi:10.3390/nu2080855PMID 22254060.
    A. Vega-Gálvez, et al., "Nutrition facts and functional potential of quinoa (Chenopodium quinoa willd.), an ancient Andean grain: a review," *Journal of the Science of Food and Agriculture*, 90(15), December 2010, 2541–2547. doi:10.1002/jsfa.4158 PMID 20814881.
    L. E. James Abugoch, "Quinoa (Chenopodium quinoa Willd.): composition, chemistry, nutritional, and functional properties," *Advances in Food and Nutrition Research*, 58, 2009, 1–31. doi:10.1016/S1043-4526(09)58001-1 PMID 19878856.
    Joel Fuhrman, D. M. Ferreri, "Fueling the vegetarian (vegan) athlete," *Current Sports Medicine Reports*, 9(4), July–August 2010, 233–241. doi:10.1249/JSR.0b013e3181e93a6f PMID 20622542.

23 Mangels, Reed, Virginia Messina, and Mark Messina. *The Dietitian's Guide to Vegetarian Diets*. Sudbury, MA: Jones & Bartlett Learning, 2012, p. 75.

than the fact that the only male US weight-lifter to qualify for the recent Olympics is in fact vegan! Kendrick Farris is proof that you can build the explosive strength required for Olympic weightlifting—he even set a new USA record by lifting 800 pounds during the Olympic Team Trials in 2016—two years after going vegan.[24] Therefore, you can get all the protein you need by going to the primary source: the whole-food plants themselves.

Iron

There are two main forms of iron found in food: heme and nonheme. Animal meat contains heme (around 40%) and nonheme (around 60%), and plant foods, dairy, and eggs contain nonheme iron. Heme iron is well absorbed (around 20%) and non-heme iron is less well absorbed (between 2% and 20%). On this basis, some expect that, because the vegan diet contains a form that is not as well absorbed, vegans might be prone to developing iron-deficiency anemia. Interestingly, however, vegans are not on the National Institutes of Health's "at risk list," meaning that vegans are not considered to be at risk for iron deficiency.[25]

Reed Mangels, PhD and registered dietician, explains that this could be for a number of reasons: 1, because vegans are especially aware of foods that are high in iron and techniques to promote iron absorption; 2, because many commonly eaten vegan foods are naturally high in iron; or 3, because vegan diets are high in vitamin C, which can increase absorption of nonheme iron up to sixfold.

Mangels demonstrates through clear tables in the book *Simply Vegan* that if we calculate the milligrams of iron per 100 calories and compare plant foods with animal-derived foods, then plant foods can be said to be superior.[26] For example, 100 calories of cooked spinach has 15.6 mgs of iron, in comparison with 1.1 mgs in sirloin steak or 0.8 mgs in a hamburger. Of course you would need to eat much more spinach than steak to consume 100 calories, but that's a bonus!

24 "Only Male US Weightlifter in Olympics Is Vegan." Rise of the Vegan, August 5, 2016. https://www.riseofthevegan.com/blog/only-male-us-weightlifter-in-olympics-is-vegan.

25 https://ods.od.nih.gov/factsheets/Iron-HealthProfessional/ accessed April 10, 2019.

26 D. Wasserman and R. Mangels, Simply Vegan, 5th Edition 2013, published by The Vegetarian Resource Group, Baltimore. 2018 revisions accessed from https://www.vrg.org/nutrition/iron.php on 3rd May.

Many vegetables in their whole-food form, such as broccoli and bok choy, are high in iron and also high in vitamin C, so the iron in these foods is very well absorbed. Indeed eating whole foods high in iron is claimed to make the absorption of non-heme iron as good as or better than that of heme iron.[27] Meal combinations such as lentils/beans and tomato sauce, or stir-fried tofu and broccoli also provide generous levels of iron absorption. Furthermore, being aware that both calcium and tannins (found in tea and coffee) work to reduce iron absorption can help us maximize our iron levels.

In summary, we can increase iron absorption by being aware of foods that are high in iron and techniques to promote iron absorption, such as increasing our vitamin C intake and reducing excessive calcium and tannin intake. The best sources of iron are cooked dried beans and dark leafy vegetables: lentils, tofu, cooked spinach, kidney beans, chickpeas, soybeans, tempeh, lima beans, black-eyed peas, Swiss chard, broccoli, bok choy, and collard greens.

Calcium

Calcium is needed to maintain bone health and for several other metabolic functions. What is important to note is that 99 percent of our body's calcium is stored in our bones and teeth,[28] and we regularly lose calcium in our urine, feces, and sweat. If we do not absorb enough calcium from the food we eat to make up for these losses, our body leaches calcium from our bones to maintain the right amount of calcium we need in our blood.[29] You might notice the effects of calcium leaching as white spots on your nails, for example. Therefore, it's not just about consuming calcium and maximizing its absorption but about preventing calcium loss. Eating alkaline foods increases blood pH and thus protects our bones from the demand for more calcium to be released in the blood.

Most plant foods are alkaline, and eating foods rich in potassium, magnesium and vitamins K, D, and C, all improve calcium absorption and protect against calcium loss. These nutrients are all present in plant foods. You can therefore meet your calcium needs on a vegan diet, and the

---

27 Hallberg L: Bioavailability of dietary iron in man. *Ann Rev Nutr* 1: 123–147, 1981.

28 "Calcium (Fact Sheet for Health Professionals)." Office of Dietary Supplements. National Institutes of Health. 2 March 2017. Archived from the original on 17 March 2018. Retrieved 17 March 2018.

29 S. Walsh, *Plant Based Nutrition and Health*. Birmingham, UK: The Vegan Society, 2012.

best foods for well-absorbed calcium are kale, spring greens, broccoli, cabbage, bok choy, oranges, soybeans, tofu processed with calcium sulphate or nigari, tempeh, tahini, and almond butter.

Omega-3

Omega-3 fatty acids are the building blocks of fat. The most important ones nutritionally are alpha-linolenic acid (ALA), docosahexaenoic acid (DHA) and eicosapentaenoic acid (EPA). Our bodies cannot make ALA, so we need to get it from our diet. The best sources of this are from consuming ground flaxseed, flaxseed oil, soy products, hemp products, walnuts, green leafy vegetables, sea vegetables, and pecans.[30] Chia seeds, too, are a perfect balance of essential fatty acids: 30 percent of chia seed oil is omega-3 oil and 40 percent is omega-4 oil. We can make DHA and EPA from ALA, although the efficiency of this process is debated. DHA and EPA are consumed by non-vegans from fish. Fish do not produce these fatty acids, however, they get them by eating algae containing DHA and EPA. Vegans can easily meet their DHA and EPA needs by going to the primary source itself, the algae and sea vegetables such as seaweed, or by consuming supplements made from algae oil.

Vitamin B12

Vitamin B12 is important for blood formation and cell division. It is not made by plants or animals; it is made by bacteria that contaminate plant foods which are then eaten by animals or humans. Animal meat can therefore become a source of vitamin B12 for humans. Vegans are thought to be at greater risk of B12 deficiency,[31] but researchers have found that nearly 40 percent of people in the US are deficient in this important nutrient.[32] B12 deficiency is a relatively modern deficiency, thought to be a result of the advanced modern hygiene techniques that wash off the bacteria from plant foods and therefore reduce the vitamin B12 content we consume. The RDA for adults for vitamin B12 is 2.4 micrograms daily.[33] The most active form of B12

---

30 R. Mangels, *Vegetarian Journal*, Issue 1, 2007. Accessed https://www.vrg.org/journal/vj2007issue1/vj2007issue1.pdf 10th April.

31 https://ods.od.nih.gov/factsheets/VitaminB12-HealthProfessional, accessed May 3.

32 https://www.livekindly.co/b12-deficiency-genetic-makeup/.

33 https://ods.od.nih.gov/factsheets/VitaminB12-HealthProfessional/.

available is methylcobalmin, which is easily obtainable from both supplements and fortified foods such as nutritional yeast and plant milks.

In this chapter we have seen that there is an abundance of evidence of good health, enhanced athletic performance, and easy weight loss when consuming nutritious whole plant foods. This is all very well and can make veganism seem like a utopia. In reality, though, it can be hard to make the transition to a 100 percent plant-based diet, especially a wholefood one! Indeed, we don't just eat to get full; there is an emotional connection with our eating habits too. If you want to go vegan, for example, but just can't say no to your mom's chicken soup or grilled fish from your favorite restaurant, then by all means have the soup or fish when you visit! It's not what we do some of the time, but most of the time that matters; we certainly can't let perfection be the enemy of good when trying to achieve our goals.

Eating vegan almost keto certainly doesn't have to be all or nothing; there is a way which can work for you! Take Meghan Markle and Prince Harry, for example: They eat vegan food Monday to Friday and whatever they want on the weekend. Others aim for "meatless Mondays," or simply plant-based breakfasts—indeed this could be a good place to start. Many around the world join forces and go vegan for one month (#veganuary) which is also a great idea as you would have a community to do it with, and a month is enough time to get a good taste of plant life without the long-term commitment. Whichever way you see it, simply including *more* fruit and vegetables in our diets can make a huge difference to our health and therefore the way we feel and look. The following chapter will show you exactly how you can succeed at eating vegan almost keto in a sustainable and effortless way to ensure that you do achieve your wellness goals.

Chapter 11

Vegan Almost Keto: How-To Guide

by Joy Giannaros

This chapter is the second of two chapters about vegan almost keto. The first chapter illuminated that you can most certainly thrive on a plant-based diet, and even if you are not vegan, making foods like green vegetables a part of your nutrition plan is essential. A plant-based diet was revealed to be recommended to many athletes, and found to be capable of preventing, treating, and even reversing every single one of the fifteen leading causes of death and other chronic diseases such as heart disease, cancer, and strokes in the United States.[1] Even simply increasing our servings of fruits and vegetables was shown to give us outstanding health benefits.[2] The first chapter also dispelled common concerns and myths to explain that we can get all the nutrients, protein, iron, calcium, omega-3, and B12 we need on a plant-based diet.

This second chapter demonstrates how you can succeed at eating high-fat, low-carb, plant-based foods on an almost keto diet to achieve your wellness goals. With stricter keto diets that call for extreme restriction of certain foods, great care and time-consuming tracking of nutrients would be needed to ensure that we get enough nutrients, fiber, and antioxidants. However, with almost keto, where the ratios of fats, protein, and carbs are more manageable and the importance of eating clean (not "dirty") is paramount, you will be able to enjoy higher levels of essential nutrients and still increase your fat and protein intake while reducing your carb intake.

---

1   Michael Greger, MD. *How Not to Die*. UK: Macmillan, 2016.

2   Oyebode O, Gordon-Dseagu V, Walker A, et al. Fruit and vegetable consumption and all-cause, cancer and CVD mortality: analysis of Health Survey for England data. *J Epidemiol Community Health* 2014;68:856–862.

Vegan Almost Keto Ratios

For vegan almost keto the calories we consume will be influenced by the ratios of 45 percent fat, 30 percent protein, and 25 percent carbs. In order to effortlessly eat in this way, this chapter will outline your best low-carb, high-fiber, high-fat, and high-protein foods, collate them all into a handy shopping list, and provide you with a one-week example meal plan. Choosing to make fat the center plate of our diet and aiming to eat foods from the shopping list means that the ratios will naturally fall into place. We will not be painstakingly counting calories or sticking religiously to the ratios; instead they are intended to be used as a guide to inform our eating habits.

While some may consider the lack of meticulous carb and calorie counting as "lazy" keto, it is unconvincing that there is anything "lazy" about it. Considering that clinical trials show around 80 percent of people who lose weight on a diet gradually give up and frustratingly regain the vast majority of weight lost soon after, it is important to find a sustainable way to incorporate a potentially radical change in our lives. The great care and time-consuming tracking of nutrients needed to ensure that we get enough nutrients, fiber, and antioxidants with stricter keto diets is quite simply not sustainable. Therefore, being motivated to eat in a more sustainable way is not apathetic, passive, or careless, instead it is an attentive, caring, and conscientious way of eating.

Before breaking down the foods and discussing them in terms of carbs, fats, and proteins, it is important to mention that our priority is to eat clean, whole plant foods, which are organic and not genetically modified (GMO-free) whenever possible. Indeed some studies show up to 87 percent more minerals are found in certain organic fruits and vegetables![3] It is also important to avoid food that clogs the small villi in our intestines, which absorb the nutrients from the food we eat so that we are able to absorb all these wonderful nutrients. Foods to avoid include processed or microwaved foods, refined sugars, excessive amounts of dairy products, and white flour–based foods.

Carbohydrates

Carbohydrates are found primarily in plant foods, and are basically made up of sugars, starches, and dietary fiber.[4] Most of the carbohydrates eaten in a Western diet come from processed grains or starches and refined sugars, rather than fiber from fruit and vegetables. The FDA states that Americans exceed the limits for added sugars and do not get the recommended amounts of dietary fiber in their diet. Indeed 90 percent of Americans fail to meet daily recommendations for fiber—this is hardly surprising as the average American diet is below the

---

3   Dr. Gary Farr, "Comparing Organic Versus Commercially Grown Foods." Rutgers University Study, New Brunswick, NJ, 2002.
4   Nutrition Facts Label: Total Carbohydrates, FDA. Accessed on 16th of April 2019, from: https://www.accessdata.fda .gov/scripts/interactivenutritionfactslabel/factsheets/Total_Carbohydrate.pdf.

dietary recommendations for fruit and vegetables.[5]

Consuming fiber is very beneficial for our health and crucial on the vegan almost keto diet. While fiber is counted as a carbohydrate, it does not affect blood sugar levels in the same way as other carbohydrates and doesn't spike our insulin levels. We don't actually digest fiber once we've eaten it, but it is immensely beneficial for our bodies and can help control weight. When eating vegan almost keto, we will be eating high-fat foods, and therefore we must

eat fiber to prevent (or improve) the harmful "keto flu" symptoms, like exhaustion, bad breath, constipation, and low libido (among many) which naturally come from eating a high-fat diet. So when selecting which low-carb foods to consume, we must choose those that are high in fiber.

The following table shows your best high-fiber, low-carb plant foods.

Plant-based fats

Fat is central to vegan almost keto and can help maintain healthy skin and hair,

Non-starchy vegetables	Fruits	Nuts	Seeds	Fiber supplements
All leafy greens	Avocado	Almonds	Chia seeds	Gum arabic
Artichokes	Blackberries	Brazil nuts	Coconut	Inulin fiber
Asparagus	Cantaloupe	Coconut	Flaxseed	Psyllium husk
Broccoli	Coconut	Hazelnuts	Pumpkin seeds	
Brussels sprouts	Lemons	Macadamia nuts	Sesame seeds	
Cabbage	Limes	Pecans	Sunflower seeds	
Cauliflower	Nectarine	Pine nuts		
Fresh herbs	Olives	Pistachios		
Green beans	Peaches	Walnuts		
Hearts of palm	Peppers			
Mushrooms	Raspberries			
Peppers	Strawberries			
Zucchini	Watermelon			

---

5   U.S. Trends in Food Availability and a Dietary Assessment of Loss-Adjusted Food Availability, 1970–2014, accessed on April 16, 2019, from https://www.ers.usda.gov/publications/pub-details/?pubid=82219.

provide energy, and help us use fat-soluble vitamins (A, D, E, and K) among other benefits. For good health, the majority of fats that we eat should be monounsaturated or polyunsaturated fats. The good news is that plant foods are high in monounsaturated fats. Plant-based fats and especially the whole foods that contain them are loaded with good fats, vitamins, minerals, and other phytochemicals that are essential to our health.

For vegan almost keto, prioritize eating your fats from whole foods such as avocados, coconut (especially coconut cream/milk), nuts, and seeds. These foods in their whole form provide much more nourishment than their oil counterpart. While the plant-based high-fat list is slimmer than the low-carb and high-protein foods, in their whole form these high-fat foods are extremely versatile! You really can make an unlimited amount of high-fat dishes, from creamy soups to nut butters, nut "cheeses," dips, and smoothies.

The following table shows your best high-fat, low-carb plant foods:

Fruits	Nuts	Seeds	Liquid oils
Avocado	Almonds	Chia	Avocado
Coconut	Pistachios	Chocolate (dark)	Canola
Olives	Brazil nuts	Coconut	Chia seed
	Cashews	Ground flaxseed	Cold-pressed coconut
Coconut	Coconut	Hemp hearts	Flaxseed
Olives	Hazelnuts	Pumpkin	Hemp
	Macadamias	Sesame, especially tahini	Olive
	Pecans		Peanut
	Walnuts		Soya
			Sunflower
			Walnut

Plant-based proteins

Protein from plants was discussed in chapter 10, where it was clear to see that all our protein needs can be met on a vegan diet. The *Handbook of the Nutritional Values of Foods in Common Units* shows that when we compare calories to protein content, per 100 calories romaine lettuce has 11.6 grams of protein and broccoli has 11.2 grams, as compared with steak which has only 5.4 grams.[6] Calorie for calorie, plant food has almost *twice* as much protein as meat.[7] Of course we have to eat a much greater volume of plant food to get 100 calories,

---

6   C. Adams, *Handbook of the Nutritional Value of Foods in Common Units* (New York: Dover Publications, 1986).
7   Kimberly Snyder, *The Beauty Detox Solution*.

but that's the bonus! Especially for those of us looking to lose weight—we will feel full and pack in even more critical nutrients and fiber.

While there are a vast array of plant-based sources of amino acids and protein, Kimberly Snyder in her book *The Beauty Detox Solution* suggests prioritizing certain protein-packed foods over others based on their nutritional value and best ratio of high-protein to low-starch/carbs and high-fiber foods. Building on this, for vegan almost keto we are prioritizing them in the following order:

① Greens, vegetables, fungi

Leafy greens such as spinach pack a nutritional punch and boast incredibly high levels of protein when compared calorie for calorie. Parsley, for example, has as much protein per calorie as an egg, and cooked asparagus has ratios close to chicken breast. Vegetables like broccoli and edamame are also great choices. Chlorella, a form of green algae, is approximately a whopping 65 percent protein. Just one tablespoon has about fifteen grams of protein! Spirulina, which is a blue-green algae, is less dense than chlorella, meaning we would have to eat more of it, but it is also about 60 percent protein. Chlorella

and spirulina are nutritional powerhouses containing all the essential amino acids and packed with vitamins and minerals. Nutritional yeast is a complete protein and full of B vitamins, folic acid, selenium, and zinc—it is a staple in many a vegan kitchen because of its nutty, cheesy taste.

② Nuts and seeds

Nuts and seeds have a generous amount of protein and relatively few carbs, but it is worth bearing in mind that they are primarily fat. They are extremely versatile and can be blended into nut butters, dips, spreads, and tossed into salads. Nuts and seeds are ideally eaten raw, and nuts are best soaked to remove enzyme inhibitors and improve digestibility and nutrient bioavailability. Hemp seeds have the best protein-to-carb ratio.

③ Soy products and seitan

Tofu is made by coagulating soy milk and pressing the water out. It is high in protein, low in net carbs, and has a mild flavor that easily soaks up the flavors you add to it. The silken variety of tofu is great for blending into smoothies, puddings and other "soft" foods, while firmer tofu is wonderful in stir-fries and other cooked dishes. Tempeh is made from whole soybeans that are fermented and pressed together. It is more dense and chewier than tofu, which makes it an appealing meat substitute. The fermented varieties of soy, such as tempeh, miso, and natto, are nutritionally favorable. Seitan is made from wheat gluten and has a thick texture that can be cubed, sliced, and diced and is commonly used in many Asian cuisines. Seitan is favorably high in protein and low in carbs.

④ Beans, legumes, and grains

Raw, sprouted legumes such as lentils are abundant in minerals, vitamins, and phytonutrients, which is why they are placed in the "Priority 1" category. Cooked beans and legumes are also healthy, high-fiber foods and are an inexpensive protein source especially beneficial for those transitioning to a plant-based diet. As they contain both protein and starch, they can be more difficult to digest and rack up our carb ratios, but this does not mean we should totally avoid them. Their nutritional benefits earn them a place on the vegan almost keto lists, although you may want to consume them less often. It is always best to buy dry raw beans and legumes and soak them overnight before cooking.

The following table shows your best high-protein, high-nutrition, and low-carb plant foods in order of priority:

Priority 1 Greens, vegetables, fungi	Priority 2 Nuts and seeds	Priority 3 Soy products and seitan	Priority 4 Beans, legumes, and quinoa lowest in net carbs
Arugula	Almonds	Miso	Black beans
Asparagus	Flaxseed	Natto	Black soybeans
Basil	Hemp seeds	Seitan	Black-eyed peas
Chlorella and spirulina	Peanuts	Tempeh	Broad beans
Cilantro	Pistachios	Tofu, silken or firm	Lentils
Edamame	Pumpkin seeds		Lima beans
Kale	Sunflower seeds		Mung beans
Lettuce			Navy beans
Mushrooms			Quinoa
Nutritional yeast			White kidney beans
Parsley			
Peas			
Raw, sprouted legumes such as lentils			
Spinach (cooked)			

Vegan Almost Keto Foods and Shopping List

As we've seen there are an abundant number of nutritionally dense plant foods we can consume on a vegan almost keto diet! Eating these foods will maximize our nutrient intake, give us energy, and help us achieve our wellness goals. They are collated in the table on the next page for a handy shopping list guide.

Substitutes and tips for eating out

You might be wanting to include more plant-based foods into your diet but just can't live without certain foods like your early morning scrambled eggs! While in the previous chapter we have seen that it is more helpful to aim for progress and not perfection, it can be handy to have some vegan substitutes for common non-vegan foods. There are an abundance of substitutes widely available in supermarkets, but if you fancy trying to make some for yourself, here are some easy substitutes for eggs, milk, and cheese:

Eggs

There are a number of delicious ways to replace hen's eggs. To make scrambled eggs, tofu works extremely well. Break it up and fry it with mushrooms, tomatoes, spring onions, nutritional yeast, salt, and pepper; or simply with a sprinkle of turmeric for a familiar eggy color. In baking, when eggs are used to add moisture (like in brownies) you can use blended silken tofu. For fluffy cakes (and pancakes!) you can mix 1 teaspoon of baking soda with 1 teaspoon of white vinegar to replace 1 egg. To replace eggs used as a binder, you can make a flax or chia "egg" by mixing 1 tablespoon of milled flaxseed or chia seeds with 3 tablespoons of hot water and let it sit for at least 5 minutes.

Milk

You can make a nutritious milky "milk" from pretty much any nut or even seed! An easy ratio and recipe is to simply soak 1 cup of nut (e.g., almonds) overnight, rinse, and then blend with 5 cups of water, a pinch of sea salt, and a couple of drops of liquid stevia. Once the water has turned milky white (30 to 60 seconds of blending), simply strain through a nut bag, transfer to an airtight bottle, and refrigerate for up to 5 days. You can also add 1 teaspoon of vanilla extract or 2 tablespoons of cocoa powder to make chocolate nut milk! You can drink your nut milk hot or cold (be

General, common categories	Vegan Almost Keto shopping list examples
Whole foods	
Fruits	Avocado, blackberries, cantaloupe, coconut, cranberries, cucumber, lemon, lime, nectarine, olives, peaches, peppers, raspberries, strawberries, tomato, watermelon
Stems and leaves (including sea leaves)	Arugula, basil, beet greens, bok choy, cilantro, collard greens, green onions, kale, lettuce (all varieties), mustard greens, oregano, parsley, spinach, Swiss chard, thyme, turnip greens, (all leafy greens, sprouts and herbs). Seaweed and algae: chlorella, dulse, kelp, kombu, nori, spirulina, wakame
Roots	Garlic, ginger, onion, radish, shallots
Mushrooms	Baby bella, cremini, oyster, porcini, portobello, shiitake, white button
Nuts	Almonds, Brazil nuts, cashews, coconut, hazelnuts, macadamia, pecans, pine nuts, pistachios, walnuts
Legumes and grains	Black beans, black soybeans, black-eyed peas, broad beans, edamame, lentils, lima beans, mung beans, navy beans, peas, raw sprouted lentils, white kidney beans
Seeds	Chia, coconut, flax, hemp hearts, pumpkin, quinoa, sesame, sunflower
General vegetables	Artichoke, asparagus, broccoli, Brussels sprouts, cabbage, cauliflower, celery, edamame, green beans, hearts of palm, leeks, peas, peppers, radish, tomato, zucchini
Other products	
Plant milks	Almond, flax, hemp, macadamia, soy
Flours	Almond, coconut
Fiber supplements	Gum Arabic, inulin fiber, psyllium husk
Butters and seed blends	Nut butters: Almonds, Brazil nuts, cashews, hazelnuts, macadamia, pecans, pine nuts, pistachios, walnuts Seed blends and butters: sesame-tahini, sunflower butter
Oils	Avocado, chia seed, coconut, flax, hemp, macadamia, MCT, olive, rapeseed, soya, sunflower, walnut
Other	Apple cider vinegar, canned green jackfruit, chilli, coconut cream, dairy-free unsweetened yogurt, dark chocolate (raw cacao powder, cacao nibs, or pre-made bars above 70 percent), kala namak, kelp noodles, kimchi, miso, natto, nutritional yeast, pepper, pickles, roasted nori/seaweed sheets, sauerkraut, sea salt, seitan, shirataki noodles, soy aminos, stevia, tamari, tempeh, tofu

sure to shake before pouring) and even freeze your milk for up to one month.

Cheese

To replace Parmesan cheese, simply blend ¾ cup of raw cashews or almonds with 3 tablespoons of nutritional yeast and ¼ teaspoon each of onion powder, garlic powder, and salt in a food processor.

To create a cream cheese, blend 1½ cups raw cashews (soaked overnight) with ¼ cup of nondairy yogurt, 1 tablespoon lemon juice, 1 tablespoon of apple cider vinegar, and ½ teaspoon of salt. You can thin it out by adding water, or even replace the yogurt with water, add nutritional yeast, onion powder, chives, garlic…the combinations are endless!

For stringy mozzarella-style cheese, blend ½ cup of raw cashews (soaked overnight) with 1 cup of water, 1 tablespoon of nutritional yeast, 4 tablespoons of tapioca starch/flour, 1 teaspoon of apple cider vinegar, ½ teaspoon of salt, and ¼ teaspoon of garlic powder. Pour blended mixture into a pot and heat for 5 to 6 minutes over medium heat, stirring continuously until it has become a delicious cheesy, gooey, stringy texture. Serve hot. You can add turmeric for a more cheddar cheese color and any other flavors you like, such as paprika, onion powder, and chili powder. (Tapioca flour is the starch extracted from the South American cassava plant and has a relatively high net carb count, therefore you may want to limit the amount you consume when eating vegan almost keto).

There are also a vast array of vegan cheeses now available in local supermarkets—you can certainly find the tastiest replacement for you.

Eating in Restaurants

There are a number of vegan and vegetarian restaurants, cafes, bakeries, and shops now which are extremely easy to locate using an app like HappyCow. However, if you are going to eat out with a group of family or friends and don't think a whole-food vegan place would be suitable for everyone, there are still a number of ways to ensure you get a tasty meal when eating out:

- Asian restaurants tend to have a relatively high proportion of vegan options in comparison with other cuisines, so opting for a Japanese place, for example, will make it easy for you to find vegan options.
- Ask for items to be left off your plate, e.g. ask for the salad without the Parmesan.

- Look up the menu ahead of time (even call ahead) and scope out what you might like to eat.
- Check out the "sides" section of a menu, as you can usually find whole-food options like steamed broccoli, etc., and can select a good variety to eat in a friendly tapas style.
- Many places now sell alternatives, like soy, nut milks, and vegan cheeses, although they may not always state it on their menu, so it's definitely worth asking.
- If you know there will be a very limited selection for you, then eat up beforehand! You can still enjoy some snacks and your friends' company without having to feel guilty about what you are eating.
- If the food looks particularly unhealthy, then order a large leafy salad and eat that first before whatever else you eat.
- If all else fails, just relax and know you tried your best!

As we've seen in the last two chapters, you can absolutely blossom on a vegan diet and succeed at eating high-fat, low-carb plant foods in a delicious and sustainable way. To see your vegan grocery list at work in a seven-day plant-based meal plan, please refer to chapter 13. It is important to remember that plant-based foods pack a ton nutritionally and are an essential lifeline for good health. So reaching for an extra serving of broccoli or having a hearty bowl of iron-rich lentil stew is way more advantageous than seeing these high-quality foods merely as extra carbs. Changing our eating habits is a journey, and eating vegan almost keto certainly doesn't have to be all or nothing. It is an introduction to your journey that simply places you on the path for long-term success in reaching and maintaining your wellness goals.

Chapter 12

Food Groups & Servings

The type of calories you consume is just as important (if not more so) as the amount of calories you consume. Due to their macro- and micro-nutrient contents, the following food groups are essential for weight loss, even blood sugar levels, and overall well-being, so we highly recommend making these guidelines an everyday goal to fulfill. It is important to note that you are *not* restricted to the foods listed on the next few pages; these food groups should take priority in your daily regimen, but you will be able to incorporate other foods as well. For a complete list of acceptable almost keto foods, please refer to chapters 3 and 4.

① Low-Glycemic Vegetables (3 to 5 servings)

Nutrient-dense vegetables are a good source of low-glycemic carbohydrates that will give you energy and help maintain

Green Vegetable	Serving Size	Calories	Carbohydrates	Protein	Fat	Fiber
Arugula	½ cup	3	0 grams	0 grams	0 grams	0 grams
Bok choy	½ cup	5	1 gram	0.5 grams	0 grams	0 grams
Broccoli	½ cup	16	3 grams	1.5 grams	0 grams	1 gram
Brussels sprouts	½ cup	19	4 grams	1.5 grams	0 grams	1.5 grams
Cabbage	½ cup	9	2 grams	0.5 grams	0 grams	1 gram
Cauliflower	½ cup	13	2.5 grams	1 gram	0 grams	1 gram
Collard greens	½ cup	6	1 gram	0.5 grams	0 grams	0.5 grams
Kale	½ cup	17	3 grams	1.5 gram	0 grams	1 gram
Romaine lettuce	½ cup	8	0.5 grams	0.5 grams	0 grams	0 grams
Spinach (cooked)	½ cup	23	4 grams	3 grams	0 grams	2.5 grams

even blood sugar levels. Several vitamins, such as vitamins A and C, and minerals such as iron and magnesium are also found in these vegetables; plus many are high in calcium and fiber! If you do not see your favorite low-glycemic vegetable, feel free to include it in your daily food regimen. The average amount of calories, carbohydrates, protein, fat, and fiber for the vegetables we provided are 12 calories, 2 grams of carbohydrates, 1 gram of protein, 0 grams of fat, and 2 grams of fiber in case you would like to compare your vegetable of choice to the ones in the recommended list.

Earlier, we suggested to eat three to five servings of low-glycemic vegetables per day. Whether you eat three, four, or five servings per day will be based on your personal caloric needs. Since everyone is different, you can tailor your green vegetable needs based on your overall caloric intake requirements.

(2) **Low-Sugar Fruits (1 to 2 servings)**
Low-sugar fruits are another source of carbohydrates and energy. In addition, they provide even more micronutrients to add to the variety of benefits the low-glycemic vegetables boast. Try to incorporate tomato or red bell pepper in your one to two servings of low-sugar fruits as they contain lycopene—lycopene is a powerful antioxidant that is beneficial for heart health, sun protection, and reduced risk of certain cancers. Please stick to the almost keto–approved low-sugar fruit choices, as the selections we have handpicked for you are the lowest

Low-Sugar Fruit	Serving Size	Calories	Carbohydrates	Protein	Fat	Fiber
Avocado	½ cup	117	6 grams	1.5 grams	11 grams	5 grams
Bell pepper	½ cup	15	3.5 grams	0 grams	0 grams	1 gram
Blackberries	½ cup	31	7 grams	1 gram	0 grams	4 grams
Blueberries	½ cup	43	11 grams	0.5 grams	0 grams	2 grams
Olives	10 olives	59	3 grams	0.5 gram	5 grams	1.5 grams
Raspberries	½ cup	33	8 grams	1 gram	0 grams	4 grams
Strawberries	½ cup	25	6 grams	0.5 grams	0 grams	1.5 grams
Tomato	½ cup	16	3.5 grams	1 gram	0 grams	1 gram

in sugar, and remaining extremely low in sugar will be most advantageous for reaching your goals. The average amount of calories, carbohydrates, protein, fat, and fiber for the fruits we provided are 42 calories, 6 grams of carbohydrates, 1 gram of protein, 2 grams of fat, and 2½ grams of fiber.

Earlier, we suggested to eat one to two servings of low-sugar fruits per day. Whether you eat one or two servings per day will be based on your personal caloric needs. Since everyone is different, you can tailor your low-sugar fruit needs based on your overall caloric intake requirements

③ Probiotic Foods (0 to 2 servings)

Our bodies contain "good" and "bad" bacteria and probiotics are the friendly bacteria which are critical to maintain a healthy gut flora. The prevalence of bad bacteria and reduction of good bacteria can happen for a variety of reasons such as sugar intake, alcohol intake, smoking, and lack of movement, so it is imperative to consume foods that contain good bacteria to ensure a balance in the gut. If you do not see your favorite probiotic food, feel free to include it in your daily food regimen as long is it falls in the following macronutrient ranges. The average amount of calories, carbohydrates, protein, fat, and fiber for the probiotic foods below are 89 calories, 4½ grams of carbohydrates, 7 grams of protein, 5 grams of fat, and 2 grams of fiber in case you would like to compare your own probiotic food choice to the ones in the recommended list.

Earlier, we suggested to eat zero to two servings of probiotic foods per day. Whether you eat zero, one, or two servings per day will be based on your personal caloric needs. Since everyone is different, you can tailor your probiotic needs based

Probiotic Foods	Serving Size	Calories	Carbohydrates	Protein	Fat	Fiber
Apple cider vinegar	1 tbsp.	3	0 grams	0 grams	0 grams	0 grams
Brine-cured olives	6 large olives	30	2 grams	0 grams	3 grams	0.5 gram
Cheddar cheese	1 ounce	113	0.5 gram	7 grams	9 grams	0 grams
Cottage cheese	½ up	111	4 grams	12 grams	5 grams	0 grams
Dark chocolate (70 percent)	1 ounce	168	12 grams	2 grams	12 grams	3 grams
Mozzarella cheese	1 ounce	78	1 gram	8 grams	5 grams	0 grams
Natto	½ Cup	186	12.5 grams	15.5 grams	9.5 grams	4.5 grams
Pickles	1 Medium	7	1.5 grams	0 grams	0 grams	1 gram
Plain whole-fat Greek yogurt	½ cup	110	5 grams	13 grams	5 grams	0 grams
Sauerkraut	½ cup	14	3 grams	0.5 gram	0 grams	2 grams
Tempeh	½ cup	160	8 grams	15.5 grams	9 grams	7 grams

on your overall caloric intake requirements. When/if choosing Greek yogurt, be sure to look for the plain options, as flavored yogurt can have as much as twenty-two grams of sugar per serving, which is comparable to the amount of sugar you will find in ice cream. In addition, the label "live active cultures" assures that your chosen yogurt does contain beneficial probiotics. If you have aversions to the above-listed probiotic food sources, feel free to skip them, but you may want to consider a probiotic supplement.

④ Summer and Winter Squash (0 to 2 servings)

Squash is mistakenly known as a vegetable or tuber but it's actually a fruit, and it is another source of carbohydrates that contain essential nutrients and antioxidants. Since the almost keto protocol requires us to remain considerably low in carbohydrates and sugar, it is important to note the lower-carbohydrate variety of squash, which is the summer squash (zucchini, zephyr, and cousa). However, zephyr and cousa can be hard to find in some grocery stores. Up to two servings per day are allowed for these varieties, and up to one serving per day is allowed of the winter varieties (butternut squash, pumpkin, spaghetti squash, and acorn squash). Please stick to the following choices, as other squashes are too high in carbohydrates for the almost keto

Starchy Produce	Serving Size	Calories	Carbohydrates	Protein	Fat	Fiber
Acorn squash	½ cup	28	8 grams	0.5 gram	0 grams	1 gram
Butternut squash	½ cup	32	8 grams	1 gram	0 grams	1.5 grams
Cousa	1 cup	20	4 grams	1.5 grams	0.5 gram	1 gram
Pumpkin	½ cup	15	4 grams	0.5 gram	0 grams	0 grams
Spaghetti squash	1 cup	31	7 grams	1 gram	1 gram	1.5 grams
Zephyr	1 cup	19	4 grams	1.5 gram	0 grams	1 gram
Zucchini	1 cup	21	4 grams	1.5 grams	0.5 gram	1 gram

regimen. The average amounts of calories, carbohydrates, protein, fat, and fiber for the starches we provided are 24 calories, 6 grams of carbohydrates, 1 gram of protein, 0 grams of fat, and 1 gram of fiber.

Earlier, we suggested to eat zero to two servings of squash fruits per day. Whether you eat zero, one, or two servings per day, will be based on your personal caloric needs. Since everyone is different, you can tailor your squash needs based on your overall caloric intake requirements.

⑤ Protein (3 to 5 servings)

Protein contains amino acids, which are the essential building blocks of muscle, and muscle burns fat, but not all proteins are created equal. It is imperative to consume high-quality proteins (organic if possible) that are unprocessed and have minimal preservatives, fillers, and environmental toxins. If you eat animal proteins, be sure to incorporate a balance of both plant and animal proteins when choosing your options (for example, a dinner consisting of six ounces of chicken, one cup of Brussels sprouts, and a side salad topped with avocado will be a proper balance of two servings of protein). If you do not see your favorite protein listed, feel free to include it in your daily food regimen. The average amount of calories, carbohydrates, protein, fat, and fiber for the proteins we provided are 108 calories, 3½ grams of carbohydrates, 13 grams of protein, 5 grams of fat, and 2 grams of fiber, in case you would like to compare your protein choice to the ones in the recommended list.

Earlier, we suggested that you eat three to five servings of protein per day. Whether you eat three, four, or five servings per day will be based on your personal caloric needs. Since everyone is different, you can tailor your protein needs based on your

Protein	Serving Size	Calories	Carbohydrates	Protein	Fat	Fiber
Artichoke	½ medium artichoke	30	6.5 grams	2 grams	0 grams	3.5 grams
Broccoli	1 cup	31	6 grams	3 grams	0 grams	2.5 grams
Canned tuna (packed in water)	3 ounces	90	0 grams	20 grams	1 gram	0 grams
Chia seeds	2 tablespoons	138	12 grams	5 grams	9 grams	10 grams
Chicken (boneless/skinless)	3 ounces	90	0 grams	17 grams	1.5 grams	0 grams
Chicken with skin	3 ounces	190	0 grams	20 grams	11 grams	0 grams
Cod	3 ounces	70	0 grams	15 grams	1 gram	0 grams
Eggs	1 whole egg (large)	78	0.5 grams	6 grams	5 grams	0 grams
Grass-fed beef	3 ounces	158	0 grams	26 grams	5 grams	0 grams
Ground flaxseed	2 tablespoons (ground)	74	4 grams	3 grams	6 grams	4 grams
Hemp seeds	2 tablespoons	81	5 grams	10.5 grams	5 grams	3 grams
Kale	1 cup	33	6 grams	3 grams	0.5 grams	1.5 grams
Natto	½ cup	186	12.5 grams	15.5 grams	9.5 grams	4.5 grams
Pistachio nuts	1 ounce	159	8 grams	6 grams	13 grams	3 grams
Scallops	3 ounces	90	5 grams	17 grams	0.5 gram	0 grams
Shrimp	3 ounces	90	1 gram	17 grams	1.5 grams	0 grams
Spinach (cooked)	½ cup	23	4 grams	3 grams	0 grams	2.5 grams
Tempeh	½ cup	160	8 grams	15.5 grams	9 grams	7 grams
Turkey (breast without skin)	3 ounces	120	0 grams	26 grams	1 gram	0 grams
Tukey with skin	3 ounces	129	0 grams	24 grams	3 grams	0 grams
Venison	3 ounces	128	0 grams	25 grams	2 grams	0 grams
Walnuts	1 ounce	185	4 grams	4 grams	18 grams	2 grams
Wild salmon	3 ounces	143	0 grams	18 grams	8 grams	0 grams

overall caloric intake requirements. If you add your own protein to the list, be sure to avoid low-quality choices that have detrimental additives such as nitrates; items such as hot dogs, deli meats, and fast food meats should be eliminated or severely limited.

6 Healthy Fats (4 to 6 servings)

This group contains the beneficial fats that include properties that assist with weight loss, increasing good cholesterol, reducing bad cholesterol, and maintaining even blood sugar levels. The average amount of calories, carbohydrates, protein, fat, and

Healthy Fat	Serving Size	Calories	Carbohydrates	Protein	Fat	Fiber
Almond butter	2 tablespoons	196	6 grams	7 grams	18 grams	3 grams
Avocado	½ cup	117	6 grams	1.5 grams	11 grams	5 grams
Avocado oil	1 teaspoon	40	0 grams	0 grams	4.5	0 grams
Brazil nuts	1 ounce	186	3.5 grams	4 grams	19 grams	2 grams
Chia seeds	1 tablespoon	69	6 grams	2.5 grams	4.5 grams	5 grams
Coconut oil	1 teaspoon	39	0 grams	0 grams	4.5 grams	0 grams
Eggs	1 whole egg (large)	78	0.5 grams	6 grams	5 grams	0 grams
Extra-virgin olive oil	1 teaspoon	40	0 grams	0 grams	5 grams	0 grams
Grass-fed beef	3 ounces	158	0 grams	26 grams	5 grams	0 grams
Ground flaxseed	1 tablespoon	30	4 grams	1.5 grams	2.5	3 grams
Macadamia nuts	1 ounce	204	4 grams	2 grams	21 grams	2.5 grams
Peanut butter	2 tablespoons	188	6 grams	8 grams	16 grams	2 grams
Pistachio nuts	1 ounce	159	8 grams	6 grams	13 grams	3 grams
Walnuts	14 halves	185	4 grams	4 grams	18 grams	2 grams
Wild salmon	3 ounces	143	0 grams	18 grams	8 grams	0 grams

fiber for the healthy fats below are 122 calories, 3 grams of carbohydrates, 6 grams of protein, 10 grams of fat, and 2 grams of fiber.

Earlier, we suggested that you eat three to four servings of healthy fats per day. Whether you eat three or four servings per day will be based on your personal caloric needs. Since everyone is different, you can tailor your healthy fat needs based on your overall caloric intake requirements.

⑦ Cheat Foods (0 to 1 Serving)

Back in chapter four we talked about *not* taking the "all or nothing" approach when it comes to your diet as you don't need to be perfect to see results. In fact, if 90 percent of all of your calories come from the above nutritious sources then you will have some wiggle room to cheat a little bit while still remaining in good nutrition standing with your overall food regimen. If you have a craving that must be satisfied (we have been there too!), feel free to allocate 10 percent of your calories to cheat foods. For example, if you are consuming 2,000 calories per day, 10 percent of those calories can be used for whatever you like. 200 calories (10 percent of your 2,000) is equivalent to one scoop of ice cream, four small cookies, or one small slice of pizza. Although we do not recommend cheating every single day, if you keep your portion down to 200 calories, you are likely to remain nutritionally healthy. Another tactic is to "save" up your cheat calories for special occasions. For example, if you know you will be eating dinner at a restaurant that has your favorite dessert, try to go for three or four days without consuming any cheat calories so you can indulge in your favorite 800-calorie chocolate lava cake! How you divide up your cheat calories is up to you!

If you're unsure of how to incorporate these foods into a meal plan, the following chapter is for you, as we'll detail a variety of ways to meet the above recommended servings in two different seven-day meal plans. You will find one-week plans for both non-vegans and vegans, and, if you want to get even more creative, the *Almost Keto* breakfast, lunch, and dinner recipes found in chapters 18, 19, and 20 include a variety of these foods.

Chapter 13

Sample Meal Plans

Now that we have talked about daily servings of specific food groups, we'll put these guidelines together in a sample meal plan in the so we can see what a realistic week of food looks like for both non-vegans and vegans. The meals and snacks found in these plans are meant to be simple, with a low number of ingredients and fast preparation time. For more variety, feel free to substitute any meal or snack with recipes found in chapters 16 through 20.

No beverages are listed with your meals; we highly recommend consuming water (at least sixty-four ounces per day) as your primary beverage; water is best for hydration as it doesn't contain sugar or additives. Other suitable beverages include unsweetened coffee, tea, mineral water, and water infused with fresh fruits.

If you enjoy an occasional adult beverage, red wine is the lowest in sugar, offering only one to two grams of sugar per serving, while most varieties of white wine contain three to four grams of sugar per serving. Soda, sports drinks, fruit juices, and other sweetened beverages should be eliminated or limited.

Your one-week sample meal plan does not include calories or portion sizes—please adjust portions based on your calorie needs. Also, keep in mind that the following plan is a guide of suggestions; if you dislike a selection of food or have an allergy, please do not consume that particular food—just make a reasonable substitution. The first sample meal plan is for those who consume animal proteins and the second sample meal plan is for vegans.

ONE-WEEK MEAL PLAN

DAY ①

Breakfast: Two- or three-egg omelet with your favorite additions (onion, bell pepper, mushroom, spinach, avocado, grated cheese). Use drizzle of extra-virgin olive oil to pan-cook.

Snack: Greek yogurt topped with favorite berries.

Lunch: Canned tuna mixed with diced celery, diced onions, and diced tomatoes, topped with freshly squeezed lemon juice; use celery sticks or endive leaves to dip.

Snack: Handful of raw pecans or macadamia nuts.

Dinner: Grilled boneless/skinless chicken breast with Brussels sprouts, and side salad topped with extra-virgin olive oil and apple cider vinegar.

DAY ②

Breakfast: Easy Chia Seed Breakfast Pudding (page 161).

Snack: One piece of cheese.

Lunch: Lettuce-wrap "sandwiches"—take two large lettuce cups (iceberg works the best to keep everything together) and fill them with your favorite protein (chicken, turkey, beef, tempeh, natto, etc.), tomatoes, onions, avocado, and mustard.

Snack: Celery sticks dipped in peanut or almond butter.

Dinner: Grilled wild salmon with broccoli and mashed cauliflower (steam small head of cauliflower until tender and mash with grated Parmesan cheese).

DAY ③

Breakfast: Smoked salmon paired with sautéed spinach.

Snack: Endive leaves or sliced jicama dipped in mashed avocado.

Lunch: Spinach salad (or any greens) topped with grilled chicken, red onion, tomato, avocado, walnuts, goat cheese, and a drizzle of extra-virgin olive oil and balsamic vinegar.

Snack: Six large strawberries.

Dinner: Lean steak topped with sautéed mushrooms and onions (use avocado oil or butter, white wine, garlic, and favorite seasonings to sauté), and side of roasted broccoli.

DAY ④

Breakfast: Traditional bacon and eggs.

Snack: Handful of blueberries.

Lunch: Salmon salad—can of wild salmon on bed of greens and favorite salad add-ons (tomatoes, onions, bell peppers, etc.); top with extra-virgin olive oil, balsamic vinegar, and fresh lemon juice.

Snack: Handful of raw walnuts or macadamias.

Dinner: Mexican platter—grilled chicken with your favorite seasonings topped with grated cheese, shredded cabbage, sliced avocado, dollop of Greek yogurt, and pico de gallo or salsa.

DAY (5)

Breakfast: Greek yogurt topped with strawberries and walnuts.

Snack: Hard-boiled egg.

Lunch: Bay shrimp–filled avocado halves—remove pit and a little bit of flesh from the avocado (eat as you remove) to make room, fill with shrimp and top with cocktail sauce or salsa, freshly squeezed lemon juice, and ground pepper.

Snack: Roasted vegetables dipped in tahini.

Dinner: Grilled turkey or ground beef burger with your preferred toppings (mustard, cheese, avocado, tomato, onion), and side of your favorite green vegetables.

DAY (6)

Breakfast: Avocado smoothie—blend ½ cup Greek yogurt, ¼ cup full-fat coconut milk, ½ avocado, ½ cup blueberries, and handful of ice.

Snack: Handful of macadamia nuts.

Lunch: Chicken and vegetable soup paired with side salad.

Snack: Two squares of dark chocolate paired with a handful of raspberries.

Dinner: Guilt-free spaghetti: Preheat oven to 400°F; cut a spaghetti squash in half and remove the seeds. Lightly coat the flesh side with extra-virgin olive oil and your favorite seasonings and place the two halves, flesh-side down, on a lined baking sheet. Bake for 45 minutes to one hour and then use a fork to shred the inside of the squash to get your "noodles." Top with hearty spaghetti sauce (a suggestion is tomato sauce with ground chicken or turkey, bell peppers, onions, mushrooms, and garlic topped with grated Parmesan).

DAY ⑦

Breakfast: Two- or three-egg omelet with your favorite additions (onion, bell pepper, mushroom, spinach, avocado, grated cheese). Use extra-virgin olive oil to sauté your omelet additions as well as your eggs.

Snack: Handful of blueberries.

Lunch: Lettuce-wrap sandwiches—fill large romaine, butter, or iceberg lettuce leaves with your favorite sandwich additions and then fold the lettuce leaves, roll, and cut in half just as you would do with a burrito. Some filling suggestions are turkey, chicken, shrimp, beans, lentils, hummus, sliced tomato, onion, avocado, and mustard.

Snack: Roasted kale chips dipped in mashed avocado.

Dinner: Grilled boneless pork chops paired with sauerkraut and a side of your favorite green vegetables.

ONE-WEEK VEGAN ALMOST KETO
Meal Plan
by Joy Giannaros

DAY ①

Breakfast: Detox green smoothie—combine a handful of kale, handful of spinach, ½ avocado, ¼ cucumber, juice of ½ a lemon with 1 cup unsweetened almond milk, and 1 tablespoon almond butter in a high-speed blender and blend until smooth. You can add more almond milk or water to thin the consistency as you wish.

Snack: Ferrero Rocher–style balls—melt 1 ounce dark chocolate and 3 tablespoons coconut oil in a double boiler. Blend ¾ cup ground hazelnuts, 1 heaped teaspoon raw cacao powder, ½ teaspoon vanilla extract, and powdered stevia until fully combined. Add the melted chocolate and oil and blend again. Cool the mix in the freezer for 10 minutes. Roll into small balls, placing a whole hazelnut in the middle and rolling around in chopped hazelnuts.

Lunch: Leafy watermelon salad tossed with hemp hearts and pistachios: toss mixed baby leaves with arugula, watermelon (cut into 1-inch cubes), and ¼ cup pistachios in a large salad bowl. Top with hemp hearts, sprinkle of sea salt, and mint leaves (optional: add a drizzle of oil, coconut flakes, and squeeze of lemon juice).

Snack: Handful of berries and a couple of pieces of dark chocolate.

Dinner: Stuffed peppers with a side of crispy Brussels sprouts: sauté sliced onion and diced mushrooms in avocado oil until the juices release. Stir in walnuts, a dash of liquid aminos, sesame seeds, cracked black pepper, a few leaves of fresh sliced parsley, and sliced olives with tahini until hot and combined. Stuff two peppers (sliced in half from top to bottom and de-seeded) with this mix and bake in the oven for around 30 to 40 minutes until the pepper is lightly tender. Meanwhile slice Brussels sprouts and fry them cut-side down in olive oil and your favorite seasonings until brown and crispy. Serve with a bowl of olives.

DAY ②

Breakfast: Matcha green smoothie bowl: In a blender combine 1 cup cashew milk, ⅓ cup thick coconut cream, handful of spinach, 1 teaspoon vanilla extract, 1 teaspoon matcha, 1 teaspoon ground flax, 5 drops of liquid stevia, and blend until creamy. Optional: Add spirulina, or use less liquid and serve in a bowl topped with grain-free granola (made with flax and other seeds).

Snack: Crunchy seaweed topped with sesame seeds.

Lunch: Shirataki noodles with black olive pesto and tempeh: Warm shirataki noodles and tempeh pieces in a pan and stir in black olive pesto until combined (blend 1 cup pitted black olives with a handful of basil and parsley, 1–2 garlic cloves, a few sun-dried tomatoes, black pepper, and macadamia nuts with a little olive oil. Keep adding and blending with more oil until you get a pesto consistency). Top with nutritional yeast or vegan Parmesan "cheese," and serve with a side of steamed asparagus and local veggies, seasoned and drizzled with olive oil.

Snack: Medley of berries.

Dinner: Roasted Mediterranean veggies, with a nutty avocado kale salad: rub olive oil, your favorite dry seasoning, and a tablespoon of oregano into cauliflower and broccoli florets, artichoke hearts, sliced zucchini, and bell peppers. Roast for around 40 minutes until browned. Transfer to a plate, drizzle with fresh lemon juice, and serve with cashew cheese dip, guacamole, and a nutty avocado kale salad (massage half an avocado into a large handful of kale leaves and combine with halved cherry tomatoes. Season with the juice of half a nectarine, liquid aminos, nutritional yeast, salt, hemp, or flax oil. Top with fresh sprouts and your favorite nuts from the list on page 92).

DAY ③

Breakfast: Sunrise yogurt bowl: Fill a large bowl with almond yogurt and top with a generous scoop of nut butter, crushed pecans, hemp seeds, and blueberries.

Snack: Your favorite raw veggie sticks dipped in black soybean hummus.

Lunch: Spicy tempeh skewers with Asian veggies: Marinate cubes of tempeh in tamari, salt, pepper, garlic, paprika, chili flakes, sriracha/chili paste, miso paste, sesame oil, sesame seeds, and nut milk. Save a small amount to drizzle on the top once cooked. Cook on an oiled grill pan for 7 minutes each side until crisped. Serve with a chili sauce (liquid aminos, sesame oil, white vinegar, lime juice, and sliced chili); bok choi, Chinese broccoli, and wakame seasoned with sesame oil and sesame seeds.

Snack: Chocolate avocado mousse: blend one ripe avocado with ¼ cup coconut cream, ¼ cup cacao powder, ¼ teaspoon vanilla extract, pinch of salt, nutmeg, and cinnamon. Add stevia to taste. Chill until ready to eat.

Dinner: Cream of mushroom soup with flax crackers: Fry onions until soft, then add mushrooms and cook until golden. Add garlic and cook for a minute. Set aside a spoonful of mushrooms as a garnish. Add coconut cream, vegetable stock, and seasoning to the mushroom mix and bring to a boil. Remove from heat and use a stick blender to blend until smooth. Serve in a deep bowl topped with the reserved mushrooms, fresh parsley, and flax crackers.

DAY ④

Breakfast: Overnight chia seed pudding: blend ½ cup hemp milk with ½ cup coconut cream, 2 tablespoons chia seeds, ¼ teaspoon vanilla extract, and stevia drops to taste. Set in the fridge overnight. Top with strawberries, cacao nibs, nuts, and desiccated coconut. Optional: stir in nut butter or tahini.

Snack: Favorite fruits from the list on page 92.

Lunch: Collard green burritos: Cook two bean burgers to use as taco "meat" (or use cooked brown lentils). Cut off the stems of two large collard green leaves, and thinly shave the thick stem to make it thin enough to roll. Top the collard green with crumbled bean burger, sliced avocado, cilantro, sprouts, sauerkraut, vegan cheese spread, sliced peppers, red salsa, drizzle of avocado oil, squeeze of lime, and pinch of salt. Roll up burrito style and serve seam-side down with a creamy nut dip and spicy kimchi.

Snack: Mojito-style green smoothie: blend avocado, coconut milk, cilantro, spinach, mint, lime, vanilla, and ice until smooth.

Dinner: Korma curry with cauliflower rice: In a pot fry onion, ginger, garlic, and chili in coconut oil until softened. Stir in curry powder and salt and cook for a few minutes. Add tomato puree, coconut milk, and 2 tablespoons ground almonds and bring to a simmer. Remove from heat and use a blender stick to blend until smooth and creamy. Set to the side. In a pan, fry onion until soft, then add cubed tofu and fry until browned. Add peas and green beans and cook until softened. Stir in the korma sauce and simmer for 10 minutes. Serve with cauliflower rice and fresh chopped coriander. Option to replace the tofu with seitan and eat with quinoa.

DAY ⑤

Breakfast: Avocado smash: Crush avocado and scoop onto a seed bagel. Top with sliced colorful cherry tomatoes, sprouts, squeeze of lemon, and cracked black pepper.

Snack: Golden chai smoothie: blend leafy greens, coconut cream, and coconut milk with turmeric, masala chai spices, vanilla, and stevia until smooth.

Lunch: Kelp pad thai with seaweed thins: Blend ½ cup peanut butter, ¼ cup tamari, 1 white onion, juice of 1 lime, 2 garlic cloves, and red pepper flakes until smooth. Toss into kelp noodles, peanuts, bean sprouts, green onions, cilantro, shredded cabbage, and sesame seeds, and top with lime wedges. Serve with sesame nori seaweed thins.

Snack: Medley of fresh berries dipped in whipped coconut cream.

Dinner: Cheesy broccoli and cauliflower bake with a super greens salad: Boil half a head of cauliflower florets and half a head of broccoli florets for 10 minutes. Blend 2 cups vegetable stock with 1 cup soaked cashews (or macadamia nuts), ⅓ cup nutritional yeast, 1 tablespoon garlic powder, 1 teaspoon paprika, and salt to taste until smooth. Place cauliflower, broccoli, ½ cup edamame, and ⅓ cup raw cashews into a baking dish, and pour the sauce over the top. Bake for 30 minutes, until the sauce starts to bubble and brown on top. Serve with a super greens salad (mixed leaves, sprouts, cubed avocado, chopped cucumbers, mixed seeds, and salad dressing).

DAY (6)

Breakfast: Eggy tofu scramble served with fried tomato and fresh avocado: Crumble 8 ounces extra firm tofu, leaving some big chunks for texture, and fry in oil until lightly browned. Fold in a sauce and cook until you get an eggy consistency. (To make an eggy sauce, whisk together ⅓ cup soy milk, 2 tablespoons nutritional yeast, 1 teaspoon Dijon mustard, ½ teaspoon each: favorite seasoning, turmeric, paprika, garlic powder, ¼ teaspoon onion powder, and ¼ teaspoon kala namak). Top with sliced green onions, chopped chives, and black pepper. Serve with a large fried tomato (slice large tomato in half and fry cut-side down) and sliced avocado.

Snack: Fresh fruit salad: made with your favorite fruits from the list on page 92.

Lunch: Cauliflower sushi makis: use cauliflower to replace rice for these delicious sushi makis. Layer cooked cauliflower rice on nori sheets, top with thin cucumber and green onion sticks, avocado, and any other favorite veggies. Season, wrap up, and slice into bite-sized makis. Serve with a spicy tahini dip (mix chili sauce with tahini and stevia drops) and sesame spinach (blanch spinach until just wilted, then soak in cold water for a minute. Drain well and toss with sesame oil, liquid aminos, toasted sesame seeds, vinegar, minced garlic, and a few drops of stevia). Option to add tempeh, seitan, or tofu.

Snack: Handful of walnuts and pecans dusted with cinnamon powder and a sprinkle of powdered stevia.

Dinner: Vibrant vegetable and tofu stir-fry: Fry tofu cubes in a little oil over high heat until brown on all sides, add sliced almonds until warm and browning; set aside. Heat oil in a wok, add spring onions, garlic, and ginger, and stir-fry for 1 minute. Reduce the heat so as to soften but not brown the vegetables. Add red, yellow, and green peppers, long-stem broccoli, zucchini, and green beans, and stir-fry for 3 minutes. Add vegetable stock and liquid aminos and cook for another 2 minutes. Combine with the tofu cubes and serve. (Optional: Use beans instead of tofu and serve with shirataki or kelp noodles.)

DAY (7)

Breakfast: Nutty pancakes: Mix ¼ cup almond milk with 2 tablespoons almond butter and liquid stevia. In another bowl, sift and mix 1 tablespoon coconut flour, 1 tablespoon ground flax, ½ teaspoon baking powder, and pinch of salt. Combine the dry and wet mix together well, and let it sit for 5 minutes. Spoon batter onto a skillet and gently spread with the back of a wet spoon. Cook for 4 minutes or until bubbles form on the surface, then flip and cook for another 2 to 3 minutes. Top pancakes with coconut cream, fresh berries, and a drizzle of nut butter.

Snack: Chocolate green smoothie: Blend coconut cream, spinach, frozen berries, cacao powder/nibs, cinnamon, hazelnut butter, vanilla extract, and stevia until smooth.

Lunch: Lupini falafels on a bed of mixed greens served with a garlicy yogurt dip. In a food processor, mix together 300 g cooked lupini beans, one onion, 80 g frozen peas, 2 cloves of garlic, 1 cup of basil and parsley, ¼ cup of pistachios, 4 tbsp of mixed seeds, 4 tbsp lupini bean flour (or use pea flour), 1 tsp ground coriander, 1.5 tsp salt, ½ tsp pepper. Roll the lupini bean mix into 1-inch-wide balls, coat in oil, and cook at 400F for 25 minutes turning halfway through. Serve on a bed of seasoned mixed leaves with a yogurt dip in the center. To make a yogurt dip, mix 4 tbsp of soy yogurt with 1 tbsp of tahini, ½ tsp of crushed garlic, lemon juice and salt to taste. Option to stir in 1 tbsp of pesto.

Snack: Raw veggie sticks dipped into a spinach, artichoke, and macadamia nut dip. Blend ½ cup macadamia nuts, 3 tablespoons nutritional yeast, 1 can drained artichoke hearts, couple handfuls of spinach, juice from 1 small lemon, 3 garlic cloves, ¼ teaspoon salt, ¼ teaspoon black pepper, and a small sprinkle of cayenne pepper to taste, with olive oil. Keep drizzling and blending with more oil until you reach dip consistency.

Dinner: Zucchini layered seitan lasagna with a Greek salad (cucumbers, tomatoes, olives, onions, and green peppers, seasoned with oil, oregano, and salt).

For extended meal-planning assistance, you can refer to chapter 16, The Almost Keto Meal-Planning System. The variety of food choices found in the meal-planning system provides flexibility with regard to food preferences, aversions, and nutrition lifestyles. In addition, they are intended to be fairly simple and have shorter preparation times. If you prefer more exploratory recipes, simply choose any breakfast, lunch, and dinner recipes from chapters 18 through 20 and incorporate your favorite snacks in between.

Chapter 14

How to Prevent or Treat Type 2 Diabetes with Food

Type 2 diabetes affects millions of men and women every year. Research shows that this condition may be prevented and/or treated through good nutrition and exercise. Since prediabetes and type 2 diabetes are on the rise, it is imperative to take precautions by implementing a low-sugar nutrition plan that is adopted as a lifestyle, as opposed to a short-term diet. If you are reading this chapter because you have been diagnosed with type 2 diabetes, we have specialized nutrition guidelines for you! Keep in mind, if you have been diagnosed with type 2 diabetes, please follow your doctor's orders and get immediate attention, as it can be very dangerous if not treated.

You may be wondering what to eat to prevent type 2 diabetes from occurring in the first place. All of the nutrition information outlined in previous and following chapters will help to lower your risk of developing the condition. Avoiding sugar, as well as consuming the proper amounts and types of carbohydrates is imperative to efficiently manage blood sugar levels. Not all carbohydrates demonstrate the same qualities and the effects they have on the human body, so it is imperative to select the best carbohydrates possible. Below are some questions to ask yourself to help you identify which carbohydrate-containing foods are most beneficial for weight and blood sugar management.

- **Does the ingredient label list wheat, grains, and/or gluten?** If the answer is yes, it is best to avoid this carbohydrate-containing food. Most products that contain wheat, grains, and/or gluten tend to have a high amount of carbohydrates per serving, and these types of carbohydrates are high-glycemic, converting to a lot of sugar upon digestion.
- **Does the ingredient label on the food exhibit a long list?**

If the answer is yes, it is best to avoid this carbohydrate-containing food. A long ingredient list is a strong indicator that the food is manufactured to a point of being far from a natural state, containing several toxic ingredients.

- **Does the food have a long shelf life?**

  If the answer is yes, it is best to avoid this carbohydrate-containing food. Foods that have a shelf life (such as pasta, bread, crackers, chips, cookies, and cereal) tend to contain a variety of preservatives in order to create that long shelf life.

- **Is the food highly processed?**

  If the answer is yes, it is best to avoid this carbohydrate-containing food. Processed foods (which are also likely to have long shelf lives) also tend to have a long ingredient list—most of which we can't even pronounce; they are not real foods that occur in nature. Not only do these foods have detrimental additives and preservatives, they boast inferior fortified nutrients that have been added in the factory and do not absorb well.

- **Does the food have added sugar?**

  If the answer is yes, it is best to avoid this carbohydrate-containing food. Carbohydrates automatically turn into sugar when digested, so it is important not to add to that sugar that will naturally convert in your bloodstream. Keep in mind that there are over 60 different names for sugar that have been found on food labels; some of the most common ones are barley malt, dextrose, rice syrup, sucrose, and high-fructose corn syrup.

The carbohydrate-containing foods that are almost keto–approved do not fall into any of the abovementioned categories. They are nutrient-dense whole foods that are unprocessed with little to no shelf lives and have no added sugars. On the next page is a snapshot of some of our favorite carbohydrate foods, based on micronutrient composition and the effect they have on blood sugar levels. The carbohydrate foods to consume freely (while staying within the general guidelines of your almost keto macronutrient recommendations) are **highlighted in green**. Also included are carbohydrate foods that we recommend eliminating from your nutrition plan (**highlighted in red**).

The reason for including the whole wheat versions of bread, pasta, crackers, and flour on the list to avoid or eliminate is because, as we mentioned previously, the truth of the matter is there is little

Carbohydrate Foods to Consume	Carbohydrate Foods to Eliminate
Artichoke	Bagels
Asparagus	Cake
Avocado	Candy
Bell pepper	Cereal
Blackberries	Commercial granola bars
Blueberries	Cookies
Broccoli	Croissants
Brussels sprouts	Donuts
Cabbage	Ice cream
Cauliflower	Muffins
Celery	Multi-grain/whole wheat crackers
Collard greens	Pita bread
Cucumber	Pizza crust
Eggplant	Sugary drinks
Green beans	Tortilla
Kale	White bread
Onion	White crackers
Raspberries	White flour
Spinach	White pasta
Strawberries	Whole wheat bread
Tomato	Whole wheat flour
Zucchini	Whole wheat pasta

difference between two pieces of white bread and two pieces of whole wheat bread with regard to their ingredients and nutritional makeup.

Traditional wisdom states that the wheat bread has double the amount of fiber and therefore will not affect blood sugar levels negatively, but that is false.

That measly extra 1.5 grams of fiber when put up against the twenty-four grams of high-glycemic carbohydrates unfortunately will not make a substantial difference with regard to keeping your blood sugar levels even, especially when combatting an ingredient such as high-fructose corn syrup.

If you have been diagnosed with type 2 diabetes and your doctor said you can manage it with proper nutrition, we have put together the following recommendations for you. There are some cases of diabetes that do require medication, so please follow your doctor's orders. If you are currently trying to combat type 2 diabetes or you are simply taking preventative measures, the following guidelines may assist you.

1 Severely Limit Sugar

The reality of fighting or avoiding type 2 diabetes comes down to severely limiting sugar. Consuming sugar is directly related to raising our blood sugar, which can result in or exacerbate the condition. Whether the sugar comes from a candy bar, ice cream, cookies, or even natural sources like honey or fruit, all types of sugar are problematic for diabetes.

2 Eliminate Sugary Beverages

Of course we all know that sodas should be eliminated, but there are other beverages that are touted as being healthy but will worsen diabetes. Sports drinks tend to be advertised as being a somewhat healthy alternative to sodas as they boast electrolytes, but these, too, are filled with sugars, additives, and artificial ingredients—the costs of these drinks definitely outweigh the benefits. There is much confusion about fruit juices in particular, because we have always been taught that they are good to consume due to the vitamin content. In addition, it is a misconception that the natural sugar coming from the fruit is unlike processed sugar in terms of the effect it has on our blood sugar. However, our bodies cannot distinguish between the fructose found in fruit and any other types of sugar. Water is the most beneficial beverage for wellness if you have diabetes or are trying to prevent it.

3 Do Not Use Artificial Sweeteners

Artificial sweeteners add sweetness to foods without adding calories. Though they have been touted for years as products that offer sweetness without impacting weight gain or blood sugar, studies are now suggesting that regular consumption of artificial sweeteners is actually associated with negative health outcomes such as type 2 diabetes and metabolic disorders, as opposed to helping to prevent them.[1]

4 Reduce Carbohydrate Intake

Carbohydrates are broken down into sugar by the digestive system, and that sugar enters the blood. In response to this, blood sugar rises and insulin is released by the pancreas, which prompts the sugar to be used as energy or to be stored in cells. Sometimes not enough insulin is created by the pancreas, and that leads to high blood sugar levels as the sugar remains in the blood as opposed to being used or stored. Carbohydrates affect blood sugar and insulin response more than proteins and fats, so it is imperative to reduce carbohydrate intake if you suffer from diabetes. We recommend an average of 75 to 125 grams of carbohydrates per day, but this

---

1   S. Swithers, "Artificial sweeteners produce the counterintuitive effect of inducing metabolic derangements," NCBI, September 2013, accessed September 24, 2017, https://www.ncbi.nlm.nih.gov/pmc/articles/PMC3772345/.

EVEN IF YOU DON'T HAVE DIABETES, this is a chapter everyone should read. The incidence of Type 2 diabetes is on the rise, affecting almost 10 percent of the US population, and it is the seventh leading cause of death in the United States, killing more people than breast cancer and AIDS combined.[2] One of the leading causes of diabetes is obesity, which means that in many cases it can be either prevented or controlled through diet alone. As mentioned here, decreasing the amount of carbohydrates in your diet is one great way to reduce your risk for diabetes.[3] Simple carbohydrates like pasta, bread, candy, and soda are not essential for life. You could cut these out of your diet 100 percent and not only survive, but be much healthier. Complex carbs like low-sugar fruits and vegetables are necessary, mostly because of the many diverse vitamins and minerals they provide. Still unsure if it's worth the effort to change your diet? Consider the fact that diabetes can affect every system in your body, from your eyes, heart, and stomach to your nerves and skin and even your mental health.

—Katie Williams, RN

range is a general average. You may need more or less based on your height, current weight, desired weight, age, and activity level.

5 Obtain Majority of Carbohydrates from Vegetables

It is still important to eat some carbohydrates, but your primary carbohydrates should come from vegetable sources as they are low-glycemic. The glycemic index ranks carbohydrates in terms of how quickly they turn to sugar once digested. Most vegetables (notably green vegetables) are low-glycemic, which means they raise blood sugar very minimally and slowly while providing energy, nutrients, and fiber.

6 Eliminate Carbohydrates from High-Sugar Fruits

Like vegetables, low-glycemic fruits are another carbohydrate source that provide essential nutrients and antioxidants while resulting in marginal blood sugar increase and insulin response. Fruits such as avocado, tomato, and bell pepper are extremely low in carbohydrates and sugar, so those can be a part of your diabetes nutrition plan. Low-sugar fruits such as

---

2   "Statistics About Diabetes: Overall Numbers, Diabetes and Prediabetes." Www.diabetes.org. Accessed May 21, 2019. http://www.diabetes.org/diabetes-basics/statistics/.

3   Felman, Adam. "Does the Ketogenic Diet Work for Type 2 Diabetes?" Www.medicalnewstoday.com. March 29, 2019. Accessed May 21, 2019. https://www.medicalnewstoday.com/articles/317431.php.

berries can be consumed in moderation (we recommend no more than one serving per day). High-glycemic fruits such as mango, figs, banana, and pineapple should be avoided, as they cause spikes in the blood sugar and insulin response.

⑦ Eat More Proteins and Healthy Fats

Protein and healthy fats have very little bearing on blood sugar, so consuming more of these macronutrients (and less carbohydrates) is key to treating or preventing type 2 diabetes. Protein and fats help to keep your blood sugar levels even, and they assist with keeping you fuller for longer, which may prevent spikes and drops in blood glucose. High-carbohydrate intake results in those spikes in blood sugar, followed by a "crash," which may lead to cravings for more carbohydrates. Keep in mind, it is critical to consume high-quality proteins and healthy fats (since not all proteins and fats are created equally). Wild salmon, organic meats/poultry, nuts, seeds, broccoli, spinach, avocado, and extra-virgin olive oil are great examples of proteins and fats to consume while items such as hot dogs, fried foods, vegetable oil, and fast foods are best to be avoided.

⑧ Do Not Eat Any Grain- or Gluten-Containing Foods

(such as bread, pasta, crackers, and cereals—not even the whole wheat versions): Grain- and gluten-containing foods such as bread, pasta, crackers and cereals are high-glycemic—they will raise your blood sugar very quickly, which triggers a substantial insulin response. The glycemic index ranks carbohydrate-containing foods with regard to how they are compared to sugar in terms of the rise in blood sugar they cause. Pure sugar is given a ranking of 100, meaning pure sugar will raise your blood sugar the most. Any item that receives a ranking of seventy or more is considered high-glycemic and should be eliminated. The average commercial white bread is given a glycemic index score of seventy-three, whereas the average commercial wheat bread is given a score of sixty-nine. So yes, technically whole wheat bread is "better" than white bread, but it is only marginally better and will still cause substantial rises in blood sugar as it is right on the border of being considered "high-glycemic." For a reference point, carbohydrate sources such as broccoli, kale, cauliflower, tomato, Brussels sprouts, collard greens, and lettuces have glycemic index scores that are less than twenty.

⑨ Do Not Eat Gluten-Free Versions of Bread, Pasta, Crackers, and Cereals

You may be wondering if the gluten-free versions of these foods are acceptable to consume while trying to manage or prevent type 2 diabetes, and the short answer is no. Gluten-free breads, pastas, crackers, and convenience foods are processed with replacement flours such as potato starch and tapioca starch. Unfortunately, these starches raise your blood sugar even more than typical gluten-containing wheat flours found in regular breads, pastas, and crackers. Even though these items are technically gluten-free, this label does not automatically mean they are healthy, as they will only do a disservice to one who is trying to combat type 2 diabetes and/or weight gain.

⑩ Eat Frequent Small Meals and Snacks

If you find yourself constantly hungry, eating frequently can help you stay full and fend off hunger or cravings. Incorporating protein and healthy fats in several small

Type 2 Diabetes Servings per Day Recommendations		
Food Category	**Servings Per Day**	**Food Examples**
Low-glycemic vegetables	3–5	Arugula, bok choy, broccoli, Brussels sprouts, cabbage, cauliflower, collard greens, kale, romaine lettuce, spinach
Low-sugar fruits	1–2	Avocado, bell pepper, blackberries, blueberries, lemon, olives, raspberries, strawberries, tomato
Probiotic foods	1–2	Cottage cheese, dark chocolate, Greek yogurt (unsweetened), kimchi, natto, olives, pickles, sauerkraut, tempeh
Protein	3–4	Beans, broccoli, chicken, eggs, grass-fed beef, lentils, natto, quinoa, shellfish, spinach, tempeh, turkey, whitefish, wild salmon
Healthy fats	4–5	Avocado, avocado oil, catfish, chia seeds, coconut oil, eggs, extra-virgin olive oil, flaxseeds, herring, macadamia nuts, nut butters, oysters, rainbow trout, sardines, seaweed, walnuts, wild salmon
Caution foods	0	Bread, cereal, convenience meals, crackers, fast food, fried foods, pasta, potatoes, processed food, rice, sugary foods and beverages

meals and snacks all day will help to keep blood sugar levels even. If you are awake for sixteen hours per twenty-four day and you eat something every three hours, you will be eating around five times per day. For example, if you are consuming roughly 2000 calories per day, each small/meal snack will have an average of 400 calories.

Contrary to the above almost keto guidelines that help to prevent or manage type 2 diabetes, many doctors still promote meal plans for those with diabetes that contain several daily servings of items such as whole wheat bread, whole wheat pasta, and cereals. As explained earlier in this chapter, these foods will only exacerbate the problem, as they will greatly raise your blood sugar despite being whole wheat.

I know it can be nerve-racking to think of possible complications such as type 2 diabetes, and we definitely do not want to alarm you. We bring this condition up because it is becoming more common and the best way to combat it is with knowledge and preventative action. Good nutrition is a very powerful weapon to use, as it has been proven, time and again, to greatly reduce the risk of diet-related ailments.

Chapter 15

Dirty Secrets of Our Food Supply

Back in chapter 6, we talked about foods that should be eliminated or severely limited from the almost keto nutrition plan. Foods with particular additives such as butylated hydroxyanisole (BHA) were mentioned to be avoided, and unfortunately, our mainstream food supply has a host of other detrimental ingredients you may not be aware of. In this chapter, you will find common additives, preservatives, and chemicals, as well as what they are used for, and the implications of consumption of the foods that contain them.

Of course, it is general consensus that fast food and processed foods can be detrimental to one's health, but the general blanket statement that they are "bad" may not convince you to steer clear of them, so we will explore some popular fast-food and commercially prepared food ingredients below. In fact, eight in ten Americans say they eat fast food at least once per month, and five in ten admit to consuming fast food at least once per week. Fast-food meals and commercially packaged foods are known to be loaded with empty calories, high-glycemic carbohydrates, sugar, and bad fats, but that is just the tip of the iceberg. If you order the typical burger, fries, and a soft drink at a fast-food establishment, you are likely to consume a combination of trans-fatty acids, butylated hydroxyanisole, hydrolyzed vegetable proteins, and artificial dyes and flavors, and these components are associated with a variety of unfavorable health outcomes.

Azodicarbonamide

One of the more recently controversial food additives, as it is used in yoga mats, azodicarbonamide (ADA) is a flour bleaching agent and dough conditioner that is banned in most of Europe, as well as Australia and Singapore. Considered to be a carcinogen, ADA is linked to cancer, neurological disorders, cell mutations, and disrupted hormone functions in animals. Many fast-food and commercial food manufacturers have eliminated this ingredient from their products, but it still remains in a variety of processed foods.

Butylated Hydroxyanisole

Butylated hydroxyanisole (BHA) is a chemical food additive put in oils so the oils can be used multiple times without going rancid. BHA is a known carcinogen, and several studies have shown links between the chemical and cancerous tumors in animals, as well as stomach cancer in humans. Many fast-food baked goods, fried foods, dehydrated potatoes, and meat products contain butylated hydroxyanisole.

Dimethylpolysiloxane

Dimethylpolysiloxane is derived from silicon and is found in hair and skin conditioners, cosmetics, and Silly Putty. It is used in cooking oils as an anti-foaming agent to prevent spattering oil, and is found in items like chicken nuggets, French fries, and fried sandwiches. In addition, it even lurks in fountain drinks as to limit excess foam you typically get with canned and bottled sodas. Dimethylpolysiloxane is used in a wide variety of fast food establishments, including ones that claim to use higher-quality, healthier, and even organic ingredients.

Dyes and Artificial Flavors

Dyes and artificial flavors are used by many fast-food establishments and commercial food manufacturers to replace real food by providing fake color and flavor to menu items. Brightly colored desserts, sodas, and macaroni and cheese contain dyes that are prospective carcinogens such as Yellow No. 5 and No. 6. Some countries, including England, require labeling of products that contain Yellow No. 5 and No. 6 as it has been linked to hyperactivity in children. The United States has banned some dyes, but Blue No. 1, Blue No. 2, Green No. 3, Red No. 3, Red No. 40, Yellow No. 5, and Yellow No. 6 still remain on the FDA's approved list—yet another reason to check your ingredients labels!

Genetically Modified Organisms (GMO)

Even if you steer clear of fast food, some of the most consumed crops in our food supply are genetically modified in order to be able to withstand being sprayed by Roundup, which contains glyphosate.

Glyphosate, the most widely used herbicide in the world has been categorized as a "probable human carcinogen" by the World Health Organization. Non-organic soy, corn, and a variety of other crops have been genetically altered to tolerate direct spraying of the herbicide, and items like wheat are also treated with glyphosate-containing Roundup right before harvest, resulting in many grain-based food products being left with a glyphosate residue. Wheat, soy, and corn are some of the most prominent ingredients in our food supply as they are used in a variety of products such as breads, cereals, crackers, pastas, oils, and numerous packaged foods.

Hydrolyzed Vegetable Proteins

Vegetable protein—it doesn't sound so bad, does it? Hydrolyzed vegetable proteins are created when foods such as soy, corn, and wheat are boiled in hydrochloric acid and neutralized, with sodium hydroxide, which breaks the proteins in the vegetables down into amino acids.

Monosodium glutamate (MSG) is one of the amino acids. One of the most widely used food additives, MSG is regarded as "safe" in moderation by many popular websites and sources. However, research has linked it to obesity, metabolic disorders, neurotoxic effects, and detrimental effects on reproductive organs.[1]

Trans-Fatty Acids

Trans-fatty acids (or trans fats) are created by adding hydrogen to vegetable oil, and many fast-food establishments use this type of fat because it is cheap and has a longer shelf life compared to other fats. When using this type of oil in deep fryers, it doesn't have to be changed as often since it takes longer to spoil. Trans fats are known for raising your LDL (bad) cholesterol while lowering your HDL (good) cholesterol. Animal studies have shown that regular consumption of trans-fatty acids has led to memory difficulties, amplified emotional reactions, and oxidative injury in the brain cells of animals.[2]

---

1   Niaz, K., E. Zaplatic, and J. Spoor. "Extensive Use of Monosodium Glutamate: A Threat to Public Health?" NCBI. March 19, 2018. Accessed May 11, 2019. https://www.ncbi.nlm.nih.gov/pmc/articles/PMC5938543/.

2   CS Pase et al., "Influence of perinatal trans fat on behavioral responses and brain oxidative status of adolescent rats acutely exposed to stress.," NCBI, September 05, 2013, accessed September 02, 2017, https://www.ncbi.nlm.nih.gov/pubmed/23742847.

There are some concerns that glyphosate, found in Roundup, could be correlated with a variety of serious ailments such as celiac disease.[3] Many studies have also indicated that glyphosate exposure may cause DNA damage and cancer in humans.[4] In 2018, a terminally ill California man was awarded $289 million as a result of a jury concluding that Monsanto's glyphosate-containing Roundup caused his non-Hodgkin's lymphoma. The use of the herbicide on genetically modified crops such as corn, soy, and wheat has increased a hundredfold since it was introduced in 1974, so further studies may need to be conducted to determine the outcome of this exponentially increased use. To avoid GMO foods, look for products labeled as "certified organic," as these items are not allowed to contain genetically modified organisms. Moreover, produce is labeled with PLU (price lookup) codes that are located on the sticker found on the piece of produce. To guarantee you are not buying a genetically modified food that is likely to have been treated with glyphosate, choose the codes that begin with the number 9—this means the food is organic!

Making the best food choices for yourself and your family can be hard sometimes—especially when there are so many hidden ingredients in our food supply! Of course, fast food and processed foods can be delicious (since they are purposely formulated to be that way!) so when one is aware of the implications of the hidden ingredients, these foods may be easier to resist. No one is perfect, so if you slip up here and there, don't be hard on yourself—but if possible, please avoid regular consumption of these danger foods for your healthiest and most successful almost keto results.

3   Samsel, A., and S. Seneff. "Glyphosate, Pathways to Modern Diseases II: Celiac Sprue and Gluten Intolerance." NCBI. December 2013. Accessed May 11, 2019. https://www.ncbi.nlm.nih.gov/pmc/articles/PMC3945755/.

4   Koller, VJ, M. Furhacker, A. Nersesyan, M. Misik, M. Eisenbauer, and S. Knasmueller. "Cytotoxic and DNA-damaging Properties of Glyphosate and Roundup in Human-derived Buccal Epithelial Cells." NCBI. May 2012. Accessed May 11, 2019. https://www.ncbi.nlm.nih.gov/pubmed/22331240.

Chapter 16

Almost Keto Meal-Planning System

The almost keto meal-planning system is your simple guide to daily food recommendations that can be used when you need quick and simple ideas for breakfast, lunch, dinner, and snacks. You may be wondering—do I use the meal-planning system or the recipes found in the following chapters? The answer is both! The meal-planning system found in this chapter is a road map of basic food choices to follow and it's specifically designed for those who don't have time for recipes. If you find yourself on a lazy Sunday where you do have some time to experiment, feel free to try the fancier breakfast, lunch, and dinner recipes found in the following three chapters.

Unlike the typical, rigid meal plan, the almost keto meal-planning system gives you several options for breakfast, lunch, dinner, beverages, and snacks—many are vegetarian and vegan-friendly as well! At the beginning of each section, you will be given a set of directions that will explain possible food options for that particular meal or snack. This will allow for some flexibility with regard to your taste buds, how hungry you are, caloric needs, and what you have in the pantry or refrigerator. The almost keto meal-planning system is based on simplicity, convenience, and foods that are sound with regard to overall health, as well as weight loss. If you are feeling more adventurous, feel free to substitute any meal with one of the delicious recipes found in chapters 17, 18, and 19. Or you can even create your own unique daily food plans using the breakfast, lunch, and dinner recipes found in those chapters, as all meals exhibited provide dense nutrition, which follows the almost keto protocol.

The items listed in the meal-planning system are easily found in most grocery stores and the majority of the instructions (we won't even call them recipes) are easy, not calling for too many ingredients

or too much preparation. If you're unsure of the appropriate serving size, the nutrition label of a particular food will list how much of the item should be consumed for one serving, or you can refer to the serving-size chart. Your caloric needs will differ based on your gender, height, current weight, desired weight, and activity level. The following visual measurement chart provides the average serving sizes of particular foods.

Serving of vegetables = a softball
Serving of fruit = a tennis ball
Serving of nuts = a golf ball
Serving of nut butter = a ping-pong ball
Serving of green salad = a softball
Teaspoon of healthy oil = 2 thumbs
Serving of meat, poultry, or fish = 2 decks of cards
Serving of cheese = 4 stacked dice
Serving of yogurt or cottage cheese = a small fist

How to Meal Plan—Breakfast

Choose one item from Category One and one item from Category Two. If you only want one item total, choose it from either category. If choosing two items, do not make both selections from the same category.

CATEGORY ONE SELECTIONS

Strawberries: 6–8 medium strawberries.

Blueberries: ½–¾ cup fresh blueberries.

Raspberries: ½–¾ cup fresh raspberries.

Blackberries: ½–¾ cup fresh blackberries.

Mixed Berries: 1 cup of mixed strawberries, blueberries, raspberries, and blackberries.

Tomato and Avocado Salad: Diced tomato and avocado tossed with extra-virgin olive oil, salt, and pepper.

Yogurt Parfait: Greek yogurt topped with berries of choice and crushed nuts.

Cottage Cheese and Berries: Small bowl of cottage cheese topped with berries of choice.

Vegan Yogurt with Berries: Coconut or almond yogurt topped with berries of choice.

CATEGORY TWO SELECTIONS

One or Two Eggs Your Way: Choose your favorite preparation style—boiled, poached, scrambled, over-easy, or sunny-side up. When opting for scrambled, over-easy, or sunny-side up, use extra-virgin olive oil.

One or Two Eggs Your Way with Smoked Salmon: Choose your favorite egg preparation style and pair with two to three ounces of smoked salmon.

One or Two Eggs Your Way with Bacon: Choose your favorite egg preparation style and pair with two to three slices of uncured, nitrate-free bacon.

Quick & Easy Scramble: Using extra-virgin olive and your favorite seasonings, sauté diced onions, diced bell peppers, and mushrooms in a pan for five minutes or until tender. In a separate bowl, scramble two eggs and then pour on top of the sautéed onions, bell peppers, and mushrooms. Cook through to your liking, gently folding and scrambling the eggs with the onions, bell peppers, and mushrooms. Sprinkle your favorite cheese on top (optional).

Breakfast Sandwich Scramble: Pan-cook two slices of nitrate-free bacon, chop, and add to a small bowl. Add two raw eggs to the same bowl and scramble. Using extra-virgin olive oil, pan-cook the egg/bacon mixture until cooked through. Top with grated cheddar cheese and sliced avocado.

Spinach and Cheese Omelet: Using extra-virgin olive oil and your favorite seasonings, sauté a handful of fresh spinach in a small pan for five minutes or until wilted down. In a separate bowl, beat two eggs together and then pour egg mixture on top of the spinach. Cook on low-medium heat for three minutes. Place your favorite cheese on top of the cooking egg mixture. Using a spatula, fold one half of your omelet over and cook for another five minutes or until cooked through to your liking.

Tempeh Scramble: Using extra-virgin olive oil and your favorite seasonings, sauté sliced onions and bell peppers for five minutes; add sliced mushrooms to the pan, and cook for a few more minutes until everything is somewhat tender. Add crumbled tempeh and continue to cook for three minutes. Stir in halved cherry tomatoes and serve.

Snack Pack Meal: 1 hard-boiled egg, raw pecans, Greek yogurt topped with berries, and diced tomato and avocado tossed with extra-virgin olive oil and apple cider vinegar.

Tuna Salad Snack Pack: Mix 1 can of tuna (packed in water) with extra-virgin olive oil, diced celery, onion, tomato, avocado, black pepper, mustard, and lemon juice (use endive leaves or celery sticks to dip), 1 string cheese, and a handful of strawberries.

Vegan Snack Pack: Your favorite vegetables dipped in mashed avocado, macadamia nuts, almond or coconut yogurt topped with your favorite berries.

Taco Lettuce-Wrap "Sandwiches": Fill large lettuce leaves with chunks of chicken, dollop of Greek yogurt, salsa, sliced avocado, shredded cheese, and cilantro.

Vegan Taco Lettuce-Wrap "Sandwiches": Fill large lettuce leaves with tempeh, salsa, sliced avocado, dollop of almond yogurt, and cilantro.

Lettuce-Wrap "Sandwiches" Your Way: Fill large lettuce leaves with your favorite sandwich items. Suggested: turkey breast, chicken breast, lean beef, canned tuna, canned salmon, fish, shrimp, tempeh, tomato, avocado, onion, shredded cheese, Greek yogurt, red salsa, green salsa, extra-virgin olive oil, balsamic vinegar, lemon, lime, and fresh herbs.

Protein-Packed Vegan Greens and Bean Salad: In a large bowl, combine raw spinach, sprouts, diced tomatoes, red onion, avocado, broccoli florets, and green beans. Thoroughly toss with extra-virgin olive oil, freshly squeezed lemon juice, and apple cider vinegar.

Mexican Platter: Pan-cook cubed boneless skinless chicken breasts with extra-virgin olive oil and favorite low-sodium taco seasoning. Plate with a side of black beans topped with shredded cheese, side of shredded lettuce or cabbage, dollop of Greek yogurt, salsa, sliced avocado, and cilantro.

The Works Salad: Mixed greens topped with your favorite protein (chicken, fish, shellfish, canned tuna, turkey, lean beef), diced tomatoes, diced onions, avocado, and shredded cheese. Top with extra-virgin olive oil and balsamic vinegar.

Protein Soup and Salad: Your favorite high-protein soup (vegetable beef, and chicken and vegetable) paired with mixed green salad topped with your favorite salad dressing (see chapter 21 for salad dressing recipes).

Guilt-Free Spaghetti: Cut a whole spaghetti squash in half, scoop out stringy pieces and seeds, and place halves facedown on a baking sheet and bake for 35 to 50 minutes or until tender. Using a fork, shred the flesh of the cooked squash into "noodles" and top with your favorite spaghetti sauce and grated Parmesan cheese.

Turkey Burger: Grill or pan-cook ground turkey burger with extra-virgin olive oil and your favorite seasonings. Top with a slice of your favorite cheese, lettuce leaves, sliced tomato, avocado, and mustard.

Simple Protein and Vegetables: Your favorite lean protein paired with your choice of green vegetables.

How to Meal Plan—Dinner

Choose up to two items from Category One (at least one selection must be green) *or* choose one item from Category One (must be green) *and* one item from Category Three. Also choose one item from Category Two (non-vegan proteins) *or* one item from Category Three (vegan proteins).

CATEGORY ONE SELECTIONS

Grilled Asparagus: Toss asparagus in extra-virgin olive oil, garlic, and black pepper; grill on BBQ or in pan until tender; top with freshly squeezed lemon juice.

Sautéed Brussels Sprouts: Slice sprouts in half and remove stem. Pan-sauté with extra-virgin olive oil, garlic, black pepper, and minced onion (optional) until tender; top with freshly squeezed lemon juice.

Fancy Mixed Greens Salad: Mixed greens of choice tossed with dried cranberries, diced red onions, crushed walnuts, diced tomatoes, goat cheese, and sliced avocado. Top with your favorite salad dressing (see chapter 21).

Simple Mixed Greens: Mixed greens of choice tossed with diced onions and tomatoes; top with extra-virgin olive oil and balsamic vinegar.

Caprese Salad: Two thick slices of tomato topped with two slices of mozzarella, basil leaves, extra-virgin olive oil, and balsamic vinegar.

Fennel Strawberry Salad: Thinly slice a bulb of fennel and plate with slices of strawberries and avocado. For the dressing, combine extra-virgin olive oil with sherry vinegar and fresh lemon juice; toss thoroughly through the salad.

Mashed Cauliflower: Steam and mash one head of cauliflower (just like you do with potatoes) and combine with three tablespoons of grated Parmesan cheese.

Riced Cauliflower: Steam one head of cauliflower until tender; use a fork to shred the cauliflower into a rice-like texture.

Sautéed Kale: Chop kale leaves (or buy it pre-chopped) and pan-sauté over low-medium heat with extra-virgin olive oil, minced onion, and minced garlic until tender (around 5 to 7 minutes); top with fresh lemon juice.

Steamed Broccoli: Steam broccoli until tender; top with freshly squeezed lemon juice and black pepper.

Baked Broccoli: Toss broccoli florets with extra-virgin olive oil, garlic, and herbs of choice. Bake until tender (around 25 minutes) at 350°F. Top with grated Parmesan and freshly squeezed lemon juice.

Grilled Romaine Salad: Slice a head of romaine in half lengthwise. Spray both sides of lettuce head halves with extra-virgin olive oil. Grill on BBQ for 2 minutes on each side and top with grated Parmesan.

Roasted Fennel: Remove the stem of the fennel (only the bulb is used for this dish); slice the bulb into quarters and steam for 15 minutes or until moderately tender. Toss in extra-virgin olive oil. Roast at 375°F for 10 minutes; top with grated Parmesan when there are 2 minutes left.

Roasted Mixed Vegetables: Toss carrot pieces, cauliflower florets, and broccoli florets with extra-virgin olive oil and bake at 350°F until tender (around 25 minutes). Top with grated Parmesan and freshly squeezed lemon juice.

Sautéed Butternut Squash: Cut butternut squash into small cubes (or buy it already cubed) and pan-sauté with extra-virgin olive oil and sage until tender.

CATEGORY TWO SELECTIONS (NON-VEGAN)

Boneless and skinless chicken breasts

Boneless and skinless chicken tenders

Ground chicken

Turkey breast cutlets

Ground turkey

Pork chops

Grass-fed beef

Lamb chops

Bison

Venison

Ground beef

Wild salmon

Cod

Halibut

Rockfish

Sole

Prawns/shrimp

Scallops

Crab

Preparation Style: Choose a preparation style for your protein.

Grilled: Lightly coat your protein with extra-virgin olive oil and your favorite herbs (see add-ons/condiments chapter for suggestions). Grill on both sides until cooked through to your liking. Top with freshly squeezed lemon juice for added flavor.

Pan-cooked: Put 1 to 2 tablespoons (based on the servings of food you are preparing) of extra-virgin olive oil in a pan. Add your favorite herbs and seasonings to the oil. Pan-cook on medium-high heat until lightly browned on each side; reduce heat to medium-low until cooked through to your liking.

Baked: Lightly coat your protein with extra-virgin olive oil and favorite herbs and seasonings. Bake at 350 to 400 degrees°F (depends on the protein) until cooked through to your liking. For added flavor (optional), dress up your protein with your favorite sauce (see chapter 21 for sauce recipes).

Sautéed: Pan-sauté your protein over low-medium heat in your favorite sauce/marinade (see chapter 21 for sauce recipes).

CATEGORY THREE SELECTIONS (VEGAN)

Quinoa

Lentils

Black beans

Garbanzo beans

Lima beans

Pinto beans

Navy beans

Mixed beans

Peas

Tempeh

Natto _? whead is?_

Cooked spinach

Snacks

Choose one or two snacks per day to eat between meals. For more snack recipes and ideas, refer to chapter 20.

1 serving of your favorite berries

Celery dipped in real peanut or almond butter

Handful of raw nuts or seeds

Your favorite vegetables dipped in mashed avocado

Hard-boiled egg

1 piece of cheese

1 serving Greek yogurt

1 serving coconut or almond yogurt

Small side salad

Condiments and Add-Ons

Use any of the following condiments or add-ons to put your own spin on a meal or snack.

Salsa, pico de gallo, green tomatillo sauce, mustard, lettuce, tomato, onion, shallots, bell pepper, avocado, mushroom, grated cheese, Greek yogurt, hummus, drizzle of honey, drizzle of agave, garlic, ginger, Parmesan cheese, freshly squeezed lemon juice, freshly squeezed lime juice, sunflower seeds, hemp seeds, chia seeds, flaxseeds, raw nuts, extra-virgin olive oil, coconut oil, avocado oil, grapeseed oil, apple cider vinegar, balsamic vinegar, hot sauce, tamari, tahini, parsley, cilantro, tarragon, mint, rosemary, thyme, black pepper, turmeric, cinnamon, your favorite herbs/spices.

Chapter 17

Almost Keto Breakfast Recipes

Keto Coffee

Keto coffee is calorie-dense and will give you what you need for energy in the morning, even if you don't have time to prepare a traditional breakfast. If you're feeling like something more, pair with two eggs and sliced tomatoes, but this filling coffee can stand on its own!

Serves 1

8 ounces brewed, hot coffee
½ cup unsweetened almond milk or unsweetened coconut milk, heated
1 tablespoon butter or ghee
1 tablespoon MCT oil (P. 70): coconut oil

1. Add all ingredients in blender, and blend for 15 seconds until frothy.

Almost Keto Coconut Porridge

You can still enjoy porridge in the morning while adhering to a lower-carbohydrate nutrition plan. This delicious, hot breakfast cereal has a rich and creamy texture with the aroma and taste of coconut. For added flavor, top with your favorite berries and crushed nuts.

Serves 1

1 ounce butter or coconut oil
1 egg
1 tablespoon coconut flour
1 pinch ground psyllium husk powder
4 tablespoons coconut cream
1 pinch salt

1. Add all ingredients to a nonstick saucepan.

2. Mix well and place over low heat. Stir constantly until you achieve your desired texture.

3. Serve with coconut milk or cream.

Prosciutto Egg Cups

These egg cups can be made ahead of time and taken on the go for a delicious and almost keto–friendly breakfast. For an impressive breakfast or brunch, multiply these ingredients by six and fill a 12-muffin tin, and pair with mixed greens and sparkling mineral water.

Serves 1 (2 egg cups)

2 eggs
1 scallion, thinly sliced
1 tablespoon unsweetened full-fat coconut milk
Pepper, to taste
1 teaspoon coconut oil
2 prosciutto slices, folded in half

1. Preheat oven to 350°F.

2. In a small bowl, beat the eggs and combine with scallion.

3. Mix in the coconut milk and add freshly ground pepper, to taste.

4. Using the coconut oil, grease two muffin tin spaces, and line each cup with one folded prosciutto slice.

5. Using the egg mixture, fill each cup until two-thirds full.

6. Bake for 30 minutes, until eggs are cooked through.

Egg Bite Sandwiches

These perfect little bites are a different take on the traditional bacon and egg breakfast, and the best thing is, they pack up nicely for breakfast on the go. If you're hosting a breakfast, a platter of egg bite sandwiches makes a festive touch, and can be paired with greens or a fresh berry salad.

Serves 1

1 slice bacon
2 cups water
2 whole eggs
1 slice cheddar cheese, cut in fourths
Salt, to taste
Pepper, to taste

1. In a small skillet, cook one piece of bacon over medium heat, and set aside.

2. In a small pot, bring 2 cups of water to a boil and gently place whole eggs in boiling water; boil for 9 minutes.

3. Run the eggs under cold water to stop the cooking, then peel them and slice in half.

4. Cut bacon in half and fold over.

5. Make the bacon and cheese sandwich by placing two pieces of cheese, and folded bacon in between the egg halves and secure with toothpick.

6. Add salt and pepper, to taste.

Almost Keto Oatmeal

Almost Keto Oatmeal has taste and texture similar to regular oats without all of the added grains and carbohydrates. To liven it up even more, add anything from berries to nut butters to cinnamon; just make sure you serve it warm.

Serves 1

¼ cup hemp hearts
1 tablespoon golden flaxseed meal
½ tablespoon chia seeds
1 tablespoon chopped pistachios
1 tablespoon pumpkin seeds
½ cup coconut milk

1. Combine all dry ingredients and place in a saucepan.

2. Add coconut milk and whisk together.

3. Simmer on low-medium until thickened.

4. Add your favorite toppings (some suggestions are strawberries, blueberries, cinnamon, vanilla extract, coconut cream, and peanut butter).

Cheesy Cauliflower Hash Browns

This is a delicious spin-off of a traditional breakfast diner favorite, and the best part is, it's hearty and filling while remaining low in carbohydrates. If you're looking to add more greens to your almost keto breakfast, simply pair this dish with some sautéed spinach.

Serves 1

¼ head cauliflower
2 large eggs
½ cup cheddar cheese, grated
½ cup almond flour
Your favorite seasonings
1 tablespoon extra-virgin olive oil
2 tablespoons Greek yogurt (optional)
1 tablespoon chives, chopped (optional)

1. Cut cauliflower into florets and steam until tender (around 15 to 20 minutes).

2. Drain and mash the cauliflower while still warm (just as you would do with potatoes).

3. Stir in eggs, cheese, almond flour, and seasonings.

4. Lightly coat the bottom of a griddle or skillet with extra-virgin olive oil over medium-high heat.

5. Form the cauliflower mixture into patties that are about 3 inches across and cook on each side until golden brown (about 3 minutes per side).

6. Sprinkle chives over the Greek yogurt and use as a dip for the hash browns.

Portobello Eggs Benedict

This low-carb take on Eggs Benedict is delicious and hearty, using a thick portobello mushroom as your base. The combination of flavors found in the cheese, tomato, and egg yolk sure won't have you skimping on taste, or nutrients. To brighten this rich dish up, chopped scallions and freshly squeezed lemon juice can be sprinkled on top.

Serves 1–2

2 medium-large portobello mushroom caps, stems removed
½ bunch asparagus, stems trimmed and sliced lengthwise
2 (½ inch) thick slices tomato
2 tablespoons extra-virgin olive oil
2 small garlic cloves, finely minced
Salt, to taste
Pepper, to taste
6 small cubes Feta cheese
1 tablespoon freshly squeezed lemon juice
2 large eggs
1 tablespoon chopped chives, for serving

1. Heat broiler and brush the mushroom caps, asparagus, and tomato with extra-virgin olive oil and minced garlic and season with a few pinches of salt and pepper.

2. Place mushroom caps (stems down) on a baking sheet and broil for 5 minutes. Flip the mushrooms and add the asparagus spears to the sheet. Broil for an additional 3 minutes and then add the tomato slices and broil for 2 more minutes. Remove the baking sheet from the oven and set aside.

3. Bring a shallow pan of salted water to a gentle simmer.

4. Carefully crack each of the eggs into the water and let sit for 5 to 7 minutes (depending on how runny you like your yolks), then carefully remove from the pan using a slotted spoon.

5. Top each mushroom with a few asparagus spears and a poached egg.

6. Top each egg with feta cheese, sprinkle of pepper, and chopped chives.

Goat Cheese Eggs with Asparagus

This dish adds a bit of flair and flavor to the typical scrambled egg breakfast and offers a variety of protein, quality fats, and micronutrients. For an added touch, top the eggs with your favorite fresh herbs and pair the dish with berries.

Serves 1

3 asparagus spears, rough ends removed
2 whole eggs
1 tablespoon avocado oil
1 tablespoon goat cheese
Salt, to taste
Pepper, to taste
Freshly chopped dill (optional)

1. In a small skillet, heat 2 tablespoons of water over medium-high heat.

2. Place asparagus in skillet, cover, and steam until the asparagus is tender, about 5 to 7 minutes.

3. Plate the asparagus and set aside.

4. In a small bowl, beat the eggs.

5. Remove any leftover water from the skillet, add avocado oil, and heat over medium heat.

6. Add the eggs and cook for 3 minutes while moving the egg mixture with a spatula on a regular basis.

7. Add the goat cheese to the partially cooked eggs, folding the cheese into the eggs until eggs are cooked through to your liking and the goat cheese is melted.

8. Serve on top or alongside asparagus, and add salt and pepper, to taste, as well as fresh herbs.

Grain-Free Breakfast Granola

If you're looking for a cereal replacement that is devoid of grains and filled with protein and healthy fat, Grain-Free Breakfast Granola can be topped with your choice of nondairy milk and berries. If you prefer a yogurt parfait, double this recipe for enough granola to also use for another morning in the following recipe.

Serves 3 (½ cup per serving)

½ cup raw macadamia nuts
½ cup raw walnuts
¼ cup cacao nibs
2 tablespoons unsweetened coconut flakes
1 teaspoon vanilla extract
1 teaspoon ground cinnamon
¼ teaspoon salt
2 tablespoons coconut oil, melted

1. Preheat the oven to 325°F.

2. Line a baking sheet with parchment paper.

3. Chop the macadamia nuts and walnuts into small pieces with a food processor or knife.

4. Combine the macadamia nuts, walnuts, cacao nibs, coconut, vanilla, cinnamon, and salt in a medium bowl.

5. Add the coconut oil and mix well.

6. Spread the granola onto the parchment-lined baking sheet and spread evenly into one layer.

7. Bake for 15 minutes or until the granola is toasted at the bottom and fragrant. Keep a close watch and stir frequently, as it may burn.

8. Let the granola cool and serve with your favorite nondairy milk.

Breakfast Snack Pack

Sometimes you just don't have time to sit down to a hot breakfast, so why not pack it to go? This easy-to-make sautéed spinach and egg platter will be kept warm until you reach your morning destination, and having some reusable containers on hand makes it that much easier to ensure you're getting a nutritious breakfast even on the go.

1 tablespoon extra-virgin olive oil
1 cup raw spinach
2 whole eggs
½ avocado, sliced
2 ounces smoked salmon
1 slice cheese (optional)
Handful raw nuts (optional)

1. Using extra-virgin olive oil, sauté the spinach for 5 minutes or until tender and place in your container.

2. Beat the eggs in a small bowl and cook over medium in the same pan for 5 minutes or until cooked through to your liking and place next to spinach in breakfast box.

3. Top with sliced avocado, and add salmon to another section of the breakfast box.

4. Add cheese and nuts (optional).

Spinach, Tomato, and Cheddar Frittata

A frittata is simply a crustless quiche, so if you like a decadent way to start the morning, this spinach, tomato, and cheesy frittata will do the trick. If you're looking for the true French experience, add some mixed greens and a drizzle of extra-virgin olive oil. For that added touch, one glass of champagne is low enough in sugar to stick to your almost keto plan.

Serves 5

8 large eggs
¼ cup unsweetened almond milk
2 tablespoons extra-virgin olive oil
6 ounces baby spinach
1 cup grape tomatoes, sliced in half, separated
½ cup shredded cheddar cheese
Salt, to taste
Pepper, to taste

1. Preheat oven to 350°F.

2. Whisk eggs and almond milk together until combined.

3. Heat cast-iron or oven-safe skillet over medium-high heat. Add extra-virgin olive oil and sauté spinach until wilted and then add half of the grape tomatoes.

4. Pour eggs slowly into pan.

5. Sprinkle cheese over eggs and spread remaining grape tomatoes evenly over the egg mixture.

6. Season with salt and pepper.

7. Place skillet in oven and bake for 20 to 30 minutes or until eggs are cooked through and golden brown.

8. Remove skillet from oven and let rest for a few minutes.

9. Cut into slices and serve warm.

Vegan Cheesy Scramble

This tofu scramble topped with nutritional yeast is reminiscent of a cheesy egg scramble, but it's made with all plant-based ingredients for those who adhere to a vegan dietary lifestyle. Pair this dish with your favorite berries, and you'll have a vegan breakfast that is packed with protein, healthy fats, fiber, and antioxidants.

Serves 4

16 ounces organic tofu
1 tablespoon avocado oil
1 bell pepper, thinly sliced
½ onion, diced
1 cup raw spinach
½ teaspoon salt
½ teaspoon black pepper
½ teaspoon onion powder
½ teaspoon garlic powder
¼ teaspoon turmeric
1 tablespoon lemon juice
1 tablespoon nutritional yeast

1. Drain tofu from its container, wrap in a paper towel, and place on a plate. Rest a heavy plate on top of the wrapped tofu and microwave for 4 minutes.

2. Unwrap the tofu and cut into cubes.

3. Place the tofu cubes in a medium bowl and mash with a fork.

4. Heat the avocado oil in a medium pan over medium heat. Add the pepper and onion and cook until slightly tender.

5. Add the spinach to the pan and cook for 3 minutes until spinach has wilted.

6. Add the tofu and cook on medium heat until most of the water has evaporated.

7. Add the salt, pepper, onion powder, garlic powder, and turmeric and thoroughly combine so that all seasonings are evenly distributed.

8. Add the lemon juice and stir well.

9. Remove from heat, plate, and top with nutritional yeast.

Easy Chia Seed Breakfast Pudding

This breakfast pudding only takes minutes to prepare and is then refrigerated overnight if you're looking for a quick and unique breakfast idea. If you're looking for added protein and like the combination of sweet and savory, simply pair with a slice or two of bacon.

Serves 1

½ cup unsweetened coconut milk
1½ tablespoons chia seeds
½ teaspoon vanilla extract
Fresh berries (optional)

1. Combine coconut milk, chia seeds, and vanilla extract in small bowl.

2. Cover and refrigerate for at least 2 hours, or up to overnight.

3. Top with your favorite berries (optional).

Cheesy Mushroom Scramble

Sometimes you're in the mood for something a little more than just plain eggs but don't have the time to make much more. For some added flavor and nutrition, this scramble is almost as easy as plain eggs but packs a lot more taste and variety.

Serves 1

½ cup chopped onion and sliced
   mushrooms (the mixture will total ½ cup)
1 tablespoon extra-virgin olive oil
5 pieces roasted red pepper
2–3 eggs
2 tablespoons shredded cheese

1. Using a small pan, sauté the chopped onion and mushrooms in extra-virgin olive oil over medium heat for 5 minutes or until ingredients are tender.

2. Add the roasted red pepper and stir.

3. Beat eggs in a small bowl and add the shredded cheese; combine.

4. Add scrambled egg and cheese mixture to pan and cook until eggs are at desired temperature.

Egg "Muffins" ✓

Egg muffins are a combination of standard ham and eggs with individual mini-quiches. You can enjoy them hot or cold and they provide the perfect combination of protein, fat, and carbohydrates. For added flavor, some great accompaniments are mashed avocado, full-fat Greek yogurt, or hot sauce.

Serves 5 (makes 10 muffins)

1 tablespoon extra-virgin olive oil
1 red or orange bell pepper, diced
1 large portobello mushroom, diced
1 small onion, diced
2 handfuls fresh spinach
½ cup diced ham
8 whole eggs
Your favorite seasonings to taste
½ cup grated fresh Parmesan cheese

1. Preheat oven to 350°F.

2. Heat 1 tablespoon extra-virgin olive oil over medium heat and sauté the bell pepper, mushroom, and onion for 5 minutes. Add spinach and cook for an additional 5 minutes or until the spinach is wilted and all other produce is tender. Season to taste and add more extra-virgin olive oil as needed.

3. Spoon the sautéed produce into individual muffin slots on standard muffin pan.

4. Add diced ham to individual muffin cups.

5. In a separate bowl, whisk together the eggs and season to taste with preferred seasonings.

6. Pour egg mixture into each muffin slot and mix in with the vegetables and meat.

7. Evenly sprinkle the tops of each muffin with the Parmesan cheese.

8. Bake for 14 to 16 minutes until the eggs are completely set.

Salmon Spinach Omelet

Salmon and eggs are sources of some of the highest levels of healthy omega-3 fatty acids, and here you have them both in one delicious omelet. For a refreshing and mild side to compliment this savory dish, pair with cold sliced cucumbers and fresh dill.

Serves 1

1 tablespoon extra-virgin olive oil
½ cup raw spinach
2–3 whole eggs
½ can salmon, or 2 ounces smoked salmon
1 slice cheddar cheese
½ avocado, sliced

1. Heat extra-virgin olive oil in a nonstick pan over medium heat and add spinach; cook for 5 minutes or until wilted.

2. While spinach is cooking, beat eggs in a small bowl.

3. Add salmon to the wilted spinach and toss to heat the salmon.

4. Remove spinach and salmon from the pan and set aside in a small bowl.

5. Add eggs to the same nonstick pan and cook for 2 minutes or until the eggs start to set around the edges.

6. Place the salmon and spinach mixture on top of the eggs and continue to cook.

7. Add one slice of cheddar cheese and flip the omelet over in half once the bottom is cooked through.

8. Continue to cook to your liking, plate, and top with avocado slices.

Greek Yogurt Parfait

Yogurt parfaits are typically filled with sugar and additives, but it only takes 3 minutes to make your own low-sugar, high-protein version that still tastes great. You can even use this recipe if you're hosting a brunch—just alternately layer the yogurt and granola, and then top with colorful berries.

Serves 1

½ cup Greek yogurt
⅓ cup Grain-Free Breakfast Granola
    (page 153)
Handful of your favorite berries

1. Place the Greek yogurt in a bowl.

2. Top with granola and berries.

Loaded Baked Avocado

Baked avocados are easy to make, and they pack a punch of healthy monounsaturated fats—along with the egg-filled center, you'll also get your required omega-3 fatty acids. This breakfast isn't only unique, it's also decadent and filling, so you'll be satisfied throughout your morning.

Serves 1

1 avocado
Fresh lime wedge
2 whole eggs
Sprinkle of your favorite cheese
Chopped chives
Hot sauce (optional)

1. Adjust oven rack to middle position and preheat to 450°F.

2. Cut avocado in half and remove the pit.

3. Using a spoon, scrape out the center of each halved avocado so that it is large enough to accommodate an egg (about 1½ tablespoons).

4. Squeeze lime juice over the avocados and then place on baking sheet. Break an egg into the center of each avocado.

5. Bake in the oven for 10 to 12 minutes until whites are set and yolk is runny.

6. Add shredded cheese and continue to bake for 3 minutes. If you do not top with cheese, continue to bake for 3 minutes without added cheese.

7. Remove from oven and garnish with chives. Sprinkle with hot sauce (optional).

Chapter 18

Almost Keto Lunch Recipes

Citrus Shrimp Lettuce-Wrap Tacos

You won't miss the tortilla with these bright flavorful shrimp lettuce tacos. This low-carbohydrate dish is filled with all of the flavors found in your favorite Mexican dish. You can dress these tacos up with your favorite additions, such as salsa, cilantro, and avocado.

Serves 2

1 tablespoon avocado oil
1½ teaspoons ground cumin
1 teaspoon garlic powder
1 teaspoon chili powder
1 teaspoon onion powder
1½ teaspoons dried oregano
1 teaspoon paprika
1½ teaspoons salt
1½ teaspoons pepper
½ pound medium shrimp
8 butter lettuce leaves
½ cup salsa or pico de gallo
Handful cilantro, roughly chopped
2 whole limes, halved

1. Heat avocado oil in medium-sized pan over medium heat.

2. Add all seasonings to the raw shrimp and toss together thoroughly, then place in pan.

3. Cook shrimp on one side for 2 minutes, then flip and cook for 3 additional minutes or until shrimp is opaque and cooked through. Remove from heat and set aside.

4. Arrange the lettuce leaves on a plate or platter and divide the shrimp evenly into each leaf.

5. Top with salsa or pico de gallo and cilantro.

6. Top with generous amount of freshly squeezed lime juice.

Greek Meatballs

These Greek meatballs have a different flavor profile than that of their Italian counterparts, so if you're looking for something a little different, this is for you. Even without the typical bread crumb filler, these meatballs are tender and fluffy, and even that much more decadent when paired with Tzatziki Dipping Sauce (page 237).

Serves 4

2 pounds ground chicken
8 ounces crumbled feta cheese
Zest of 1 lemon
1 tablespoon fresh lemon juice
2 tablespoons finely chopped rosemary
1 egg
1 teaspoon ground pepper
½ teaspoon salt
1 tablespoon olive oil
1 tablespoon butter

1. In a bowl place all the ingredients, except the oil and butter, and combine thoroughly with your hands.

2. Roll the mixture into evenly sized meatballs (should make about 30 depending on their size).

3. Heat a large nonstick frying pan over medium heat and add the oil and butter.

4. Place the meatballs into the frying pan and cook for 7 minutes on each side; reduce heat if meatballs start to brown too quickly.

5. Remove from the pan and serve with Tzatziki Dipping Sauce.

Steakhouse Salad with Creamy Horseradish Sauce

This is a lighter and healthier twist on your favorite steakhouse salad, accompanied by almost keto–approved creamy horseradish dressing. The large variety of fresh produce will give you an assortment of micronutrients, and, remember, if grass-fed beef is available, the composition of omega-3 fatty acids will be even higher.

Serves 2

Salad:

2 (5-ounce) beef tenderloin steaks, trimmed (about ¾–1 inch thick)
1 teaspoon extra-virgin olive oil
Salt and pepper to taste
4 cups romaine lettuce, chopped
¼ bell pepper, thinly sliced
1 cup cherry tomatoes, halved
¼ cup red onion, thinly sliced
½ cup cucumber, thinly sliced
¼ cup freshly chopped basil or mint

Dressing:

¾ cup Greek yogurt
¼ cup chopped red onion
2 teaspoons chopped fresh chives
2½ teaspoons prepared horseradish
½ teaspoon fresh lemon juice
¼ teaspoon freshly ground black pepper

1. Lightly coat steaks with extra-virgin olive oil on both sides, season with salt and pepper, and place on grill rack and grill five minutes on each side or until desired temperature. Let stand 10 minutes before slicing.

2. While steak rests, divide lettuce, bell pepper, tomatoes, red onion, cucumber, and basil on two plates.

3. For the dressing, combine all ingredients and drizzle evenly over the salad.

4. Top each salad with steak slices.

Deluxe Vegan Protein Bowl with Tahini Dressing

This high-protein vegan bowl is a mixture of sweet and savory and will give you healthy fats, low-glycemic carbohydrates, and several vitamins and minerals, in addition to plant-based protein. If you're not vegan, grilled chicken makes an excellent addition.

Serves 2

Bowl:

1 cup broccoli florets
1 cup cubed butternut squash
1 tablespoon extra-virgin olive oil
Salt, to taste
Pepper, to taste
Garlic powder, to taste
2 cups curly kale or arugula
Handful shredded purple cabbage
½ avocado, sliced
1 tablespoon hemp seeds
1 tablespoon sesame seeds

Tahini Dressing:

¼ cup tahini
Juice of 1 lemon
1 clove garlic, minced
Salt and pepper, to taste
1–2 tablespoons warm water to thin
Dash of real maple syrup (optional)

1. Preheat oven to 400°F.

2. Toss broccoli and cubed butternut squash in olive oil, salt, pepper, and garlic powder and place on a baking sheet.

3. Roast for 25 to 30 minutes or until tender.

4. Meanwhile, place the kale or arugula in a medium bowl.

5. Top with cabbage, avocado, and roasted broccoli and butternut squash.

6. Combine all dressing ingredients thoroughly and drizzle on top.

7. Top with hemp seeds and sesame seeds.

Mayo-Free Tuna Salad

Mayo-Free Tuna Salad is a light, crisp, and herbaceous rendition of the childhood classic. This salad can be eaten by itself, with celery sticks as dippers, on a bed of romaine lettuce, or stuffed into an avocado half. If you prefer traditional tuna salad with mayo, you can skip to the next recipe.

Serves 1

1 egg
1 can tuna packed in water (strain out as
    much water as possible)
1 tablespoon extra-virgin olive oil
Juice from ½ lemon
1 tablespoon mustard
Handful of parsley, chopped
2 tablespoons red onion, diced
1 celery stalk (with leaves), chopped
4 cherry tomatoes, cut in half
½ avocado, diced
1 cup romaine lettuce, chopped

1. Boil the egg first (this takes the longest).

2. As the egg is boiling, mix the can of tuna with all other ingredients except the lettuce.

3. After the egg is done boiling (around 10 to 12 minutes), dice and mix into the salad.

4. Serve on a bed of lettuce or stuffed into an avocado, or enjoy by itself.

Loaded Cauliflower Salad

If you love potato salad, this will do the trick without all of the unwanted carbohydrates. Typically, potato salad is used as a potluck side dish, but this loaded version will stand on its own as a satisfying meal. If you feel like you need some more protein, pair with some grilled chicken or steak.

Serves 3

4 slices bacon
1 head cauliflower, chopped into bite-size pieces
2 tablespoons extra-virgin olive oil
2 cloves garlic, minced
Salt, to taste
Pepper, to taste
½ cup full-fat Greek yogurt
½ cup avocado-oil mayo
4 ounces shredded sharp white cheddar cheese
4 green onions, chopped
1 bunch chopped fresh chives
2 dashes hot sauce
¼ teaspoon paprika

1. Place the bacon in a medium skillet and cook over medium heat, while turning over occasionally, for 10 minutes or until cooked through to your liking. Chop into small bits and set aside.

2. Preheat oven to 400°F, and line a baking sheet with foil.

3. Combine cauliflower, extra-virgin olive oil, garlic, salt, and pepper in a large bowl. Spread the cauliflower evenly on the lined baking sheet, and roast for 15 to 20 minutes or until lightly browned.

4. Place the roasted cauliflower, Greek yogurt, and avocado-oil mayo in a large bowl and stir until cauliflower is evenly coated.

5. Fold in the bacon bits, shredded cheese, green onions, chives, hot sauce, and paprika. Add more salt and pepper, to taste.

6. Refrigerate for at least 2 hours before serving.

Zucchini Boat Tuna Salad

This is a healthier version of traditional mayo-filled tuna salad, and the hand-held zucchini boats make them convenient for a picnic or work lunch. This simple recipe is high in protein, high in healthy fat, and low in carbohydrates, and it only takes minutes to prepare.

Serves 1

1 large zucchini
1 can tuna packed in water
   (strain out as much water as possible)
1 tablespoon avocado-oil mayo
   (or "Paleo mayo")
Juice from ½ lemon
¼ bell pepper, diced
Handful of parsley, chopped
Black pepper, to taste

1. Slice your zucchini in half. Hollow it out by scraping out the inner soft layer and set aside.

2. Mix tuna with avocado-oil mayo, lemon juice, and bell pepper.

3. Fill zucchini boat with tuna mixture and top with parsley and ground pepper.

Turkey Bacon Avocado Lettuce Wrap

This low-carbohydrate take on an old deli sandwich favorite will not disappoint. This wrap holds up well if secured with toothpicks so it can be taken to work or out for a picnic. Try some celery sticks dipped in peanut butter as a tasty side snack.

Serves 2

2 large iceberg lettuce leaves
1 cup boneless, skinless turkey breast,
   shredded or chopped
2 tablespoons avocado-oil mayo (aka "Paleo
   Mayo," sold in most major grocery stores)
4 slices nitrate-free bacon, cooked
1 avocado, sliced
1 Roma tomato, thinly sliced

1. Lay out the lettuce leaves on a cutting board (one for each wrap).

2. Toss turkey with avocado-oil mayo, divide evenly in half, and place on each lettuce leaf.

3. Layer two slices of bacon on the top of the turkey in each wrap, followed by slices of avocado and then tomato.

4. Fold the bottom up, the sides in, and roll like a burrito. Slice in half then serve cold.

Caprese Salad Jar

If you're in the mood for a fancy Italian dish either at work or on the go, this salad can be made ahead of time, because the ingredients hold up well. This vegetarian salad is filling enough for a meal as it's high in protein, but if you're looking for a bit more, grilled chicken is a complementary addition.

Serves 1

5 small balls of mozzarella (sold in most grocery stores)
7 cherry tomatoes
Handful fresh basil leaves
1 tablespoon extra-virgin olive oil
½ tablespoon apple cider vinegar
Salt, to taste
Pepper, to taste

1. Slice mozzarella balls and cherry tomatoes in half.

2. Rip basil into single leaves.

3. Evenly distribute mozzarella, tomatoes, and basil in a jar.

4. Whisk olive oil and apple cider vinegar together and add salt and pepper, to taste.

5. Pour over salad and seal with jar lid. Refrigerate until eaten.

Blueberry Walnut Chicken Salad

This is a healthier take on old-fashioned chicken salad that you may find at a picnic or outdoor party. This versatile salad holds up well in the refrigerator, so it can be made in larger portions (simply double or triple the recipe), and goes well on a bed of greens, or with endive leaves or celery stick dippers.

Serves 3

2 boneless, skinless chicken breasts, cooked, cooled, and cut into small cubes
½ cup fresh blueberries
¼ cup diced celery
¼ cup diced red onion
3 tablespoons chopped walnuts
1 tablespoon fresh rosemary leaves, chopped
¼ teaspoon sea salt
½ teaspoon black pepper
½ cup avocado-oil mayo

1. Combine all ingredients except mayo in a bowl. Add mayo and gently stir to combine.

2. Serve with butter lettuce wraps, over a bed of mixed greens, or in endive leaves.

Teriyaki Mushroom Lettuce Cups

If you're in the mood for Asian cuisine, this vegan-friendly dish uses mushrooms as the "meat" of your lettuce cups. If you aren't vegan, feel free to replace the mushrooms with chicken or simply double the sauce and match the amount of mushrooms with chicken, keeping in mind this dish will now serve at least five people.

Serves 3

⅓ cup tamari
1 tablespoon rice vinegar
1 tablespoon real maple syrup
2 teaspoons garlic, minced (about 4 cloves)
1½ teaspoons sesame oil
¼ teaspoon ground ginger
3 large portobello mushrooms
1 tablespoon coconut oil
1 onion, thinly sliced
1 medium carrot, thinly sliced
Salt, to taste
Pepper, to taste
1 head butter lettuce
Green onions, thinly sliced, for topping

1. In a medium bowl, add tamari, vinegar, maple syrup, garlic, sesame oil, and ginger. Whisk to combine.

2. Chop the mushrooms into small chunks and place in the mixture to marinate; stir to coat and set aside.

3. In a medium skillet or wok over medium-low heat, warm coconut oil. Add the onion and carrot and cook for 5 to 7 minutes or until softened. Salt and pepper to taste.

4. Pour the mushroom mixture into the pan and cook for 5 minutes while stirring until the mushroom is tender.

5. Spoon the mixture into lettuce cups and top with sliced green onions.

Simple Cheeseburger

Sometimes you just feel like a cheeseburger, and, yes, you can have one without sabotaging your weight-loss goals. The majority of the empty calories, carbohydrates, and sugars are found in the burger bun, French fries, and beverage, so if you leave those additions off, you can still enjoy a juicy burger. Try using some mustard and avocado oil mayo as your spreads, and the addition of bacon is optional.

Serves 1

5 ounces ground beef
Salt, to taste
Pepper, to taste
Garlic powder, to taste
Oregano, to taste
1 tablespoon extra-virgin olive oil
1 slice favorite cheese
Handful favorite lettuce leaves
1 thick slice tomato
1 slice raw onion
1 slice cooked bacon (optional)

1. Season the burger meat with salt, pepper, garlic, and oregano, and form a burger patty. Using extra-virgin olive oil, grill or pan-cook over medium heat until cooked through to your liking.

2. Top the burger with one slice of your favorite cheese while there is 1 minute left of cooking.

3. Plate the burger with sliced lettuce, tomato, onion, and optional bacon.

4. Serve with mustard and avocado oil mayo.

Strawberry Spinach Salad

This high-protein and healthy-fat vegetarian salad will help keep you cool during the warmer months. The bright flavors of the strawberries and spinach contrast perfectly with the walnuts and cheese to create the perfect low-carb dish. Looking for even more protein? Try adding some grilled tempeh or prawns.

Serves 2

4 cups raw spinach
½ avocado, mashed
1 tablespoon extra-virgin olive oil
½ cup chopped walnuts
¼ cup crumbled feta or goat cheese (replace with nut-based cheese for vegan option)
2 teaspoons apple cider vinegar
Juice from 1 lemon

1. Place the spinach in a large bowl.

2. Combine the mashed avocado with extra-virgin olive oil and mix until you have a creamy smooth texture.

3. Massage the spinach with the avocado-oil mixture until evenly coated.

4. Top spinach with walnuts, cheese, apple cider vinegar, and freshly squeezed lemon juice.

Lunch Snack Pack

Sometimes you don't feel like an actual meal for lunch, and a variety of delicious snacks will do the trick—not to mention, it can be easier and faster to pack and take on the go. For a full week of lunches, simply multiply this recipe by five, package, and refrigerate, as it will all hold up for the week.

1 small container Greek yogurt

8 strawberries

¼ cup raw walnuts

Handful of raw broccoli florets and celery sticks

½ cup mashed avocado for dipping

2 tablespoons peanut butter for dipping

1 hard-boiled egg

1. Package all ingredients in a portable container and refrigerate.

Vegan Lunch Snack Pack

If you liked the overall idea of the previous lunch snack pack but adhere to a plant-based nutrition plan, this vegan-friendly option is for you. For a full week of lunches, simply multiply this recipe by five, package, and refrigerate as it will all hold up for the week.

Serves 1

1 small container coconut or almond yogurt

8 strawberries

¼ cup raw walnuts

Handful of raw broccoli florets and celery sticks

½ cup mashed avocado for dipping

2 tablespoons peanut butter for dipping

1 ounce nut-based cheese

1. Package all ingredients in a portable container and refrigerate.

Joy's Simple Salad

This universal salad base will accommodate the favorite toppings of your choice as it pairs nicely with most foods and flavors. The avocado dressing is simple and healthy, and it provides a creamy texture that is reminiscent of more decadent salad dressings that sometimes don't have the most ideal ingredients.

Serves 1

2 cups curly kale or chopped romaine lettuce
½ avocado
2 tablespoons extra-virgin olive oil
1 tablespoon apple cider vinegar
Coconut aminos, to taste
Nutritional yeast flakes, to taste
Freshly squeezed lemon juice, to taste

1. Place the curly kale or lettuce in a medium bowl.

2. In a small bowl, mash the avocado with a fork until it forms a paste.

3. Drizzle in the oil gradually as you thoroughly combine with the avocado.

4. Drizzle in the apple cider vinegar and thoroughly combine with the avocado mixture.

5. Using your hands, massage the avocado dressing into the kale or lettuce until all leaves are coated.

6. Top with coconut aminos, nutritional yeast, and fresh lemon juice, to taste.

Zoodles Bolognese

If you're in the mood for a traditional pasta dish but want to avoid the excess carbohydrates without sacrificing flavor, this version of spaghetti Bolognese will not disappoint. If you prefer, you can substitute turkey or chicken for the ground beef. If you're vegan, you can leave the meat out and use a nut-based cheese and fresh parsley for the toppers.

Serves 5

1 tablespoon extra-virgin olive oil

2 pounds ground beef (you can use turkey or chicken if you prefer)

2 cups store bought tomato-based pasta sauce (look for ingredient labels that have minimal ingredients such as tomatoes, tomato paste, onion, garlic, and extra-virgin olive oil)

4 medium zucchini, sliced using a julienne peeler or vegetable spiralizer

4 tablespoons freshly chopped parsley

Grated Parmesan cheese, to taste

1. Using extra-virgin olive oil, cook the ground beef (or turkey or chicken) in a pan over medium-high heat for 8 minutes until browned on all sides.

2. Add pasta sauce and continue to cook on medium heat for 3 to 5 minutes or until cooked through. Transfer to a bowl when done.

3. While your meat sauce is cooking, use a spiralizer to create your zoodles (zucchini noodles). If you do not have a spiralizer, you can use a julienne peeler to peel the zucchini all around until you get to the soft center.

4. Using the same pan in which you prepared the meat sauce, cook the zoodles over medium heat for 3 to 5 minutes until you reach desired tenderness. Add the meat sauce back into the pan and combine with the zoodles or plate the zoodles and top with meat sauce. Top with fresh parsley and grated Parmesan cheese.

Chapter 19

Almost Keto Dinner Recipes

Pesto Shrimp Scampi

Summer squash (or zucchini) is a popular low-carb "noodle" option that will allow you to enjoy your favorite pasta flavors. This light dish is perfect for a summer evening, and even if you don't have a spiralizer (to prepare the zoodles [zucchini noodles]), simply use a knife, vegetable peeler, or grater.

Serves 2

2 summer squash or zucchini
2 tablespoons butter
¼ cup chicken broth
½ cup pesto
2 tablespoons freshly squeezed lemon juice
⅛ teaspoon red chili flakes
1 pound shrimp
Salt, to taste
Pepper, to taste
2 tablespoons parsley, chopped
Grated Parmesan cheese, to taste

1. Prepare your zoodles with a spiralizer or vegetable peeler. Spread the zoodles out on a paper towel and set aside for 20 minutes.

2. In a large pan, melt the butter over medium heat. Add the chicken broth, pesto, lemon juice, and red chili flakes. Bring to a light bowl, then add the shrimp.

3. Continue to simmer until the shrimp begin to turn pink, and reduce heat to low. Add salt and pepper, to taste.

4. Place the zoodles in the pan and toss thoroughly until zoodles are coated with the shrimp scampi sauce.

5. Plate and top with fresh parsley and grated Parmesan.

Slow-Cooker Taco Soup

You'll get all of the Mexican flavors found in a traditional meal right in one slow cooker! Not to mention, this low-carb version is full of flavor, and you can simply prepare the ground beef or turkey ahead of time and place all ingredients in the slow cooker, letting it prepare itself in time for dinner.

Serves 4-6

2 pounds ground beef or ground turkey
8 ounces cream cheese
20 ounces jarred or canned diced tomatoes
4 cloves garlic, minced
1 tablespoon onion flakes
2 tablespoons chili powder
2 teaspoons cumin
Salt, to taste
Pepper, to taste
32 ounces beef broth
½ cup heavy cream
Greek yogurt (optional)
Shredded cheese (optional)
Sliced avocado (optional)
Diced tomatoes (optional)
Diced onions (optional)
Cilantro (optional)

1. Brown ground beef or turkey until fully cooked.

2. While meat is browning, place cream cheese, jarred tomatoes, garlic, onion flakes, chili powder, cumin, salt, and pepper in the slow cooker.

3. Drain grease off ground beef or turkey and place in the slow cooker. Stir to combine with cream cheese and tomato mixture.

4. Add beef broth and stir to combine.

5. Cook on low for 4 hours or high for 2 hours.

6. Garnish with suggested toppings of your choice.

Vegan Alfredo

This rich and cheesy dish is filled with fresh produce and a vegan-friendly sauce that even non-vegans will love. If you're in a pasta mood, this cheese sauce goes wonderfully with zucchini noodles or shirataki noodles and, of course, if you eat animal proteins, chicken is a delicious addition.

Serves 4

1 tablespoon avocado oil
1 bell pepper, sliced
½ onion, sliced
8 mushrooms, sliced
2 stalks celery, chopped
1 cup broccoli, chopped into smaller florets
¾ cup raw cashew pieces
2 tablespoons nutritional yeast flakes
1 teaspoon salt
¼ teaspoon garlic powder
3 tablespoons lemon juice
⅓ cup water

1. In a large pan, add avocado oil and place over medium heat.

2. Add all sliced and chopped produce; stir and toss continually so none burn.

3. While the produce mixture is cooking, in a food processor or blender, process the cashews to a very fine powder (add a drizzle of water if needed).

4. Add nutritional yeast, salt, and garlic powder and combine.

5. Add lemon juice and water and blend until smooth.

6. Once the vegetables are cooked till tender, poor the cheese sauce in the pan and toss. Plate and serve.

Shirataki Spaghetti and Meatballs

If you're in the mood for some old-fashioned spaghetti and meatballs, this almost keto version will not disappoint. Shirataki noodles are extremely low in carbohydrates and high in fiber, and this hearty dish with meatballs and spaghetti sauce stands up on its own or can be paired with a side salad.

Serves 4

1 pound ground pork
1 pound ground beef
2 eggs
¼ cup shredded Parmesan
2 tablespoons Italian seasoning, divided
Salt, to taste
Pepper, to taste
15 ounce jar or can tomato sauce
1 teaspoon onion powder
28 ounces shirataki noodles

1. Preheat oven to 375°F.

2. In a large bowl, combine the ground pork, beef, eggs, and Parmesan, 1 tablespoon Italian seasoning, salt, and pepper.

3. Form into small balls (around 40) and place on a foil-lined baking sheet; bake for 15 to 20 minutes until fully cooked.

4. Add tomato sauce, onion powder, and salt and pepper, to taste (optional) to a large saucepan and bring to a boil. Reduce heat to low.

5. Prepare the shirataki noodles according to the package instructions.

6. Add the cooked meatballs to the sauce and thoroughly toss until all meatballs are coated.

7. Drain the noodles and top with the meatballs and sauce. Add extra Parmesan and fresh parsley if desired.

Simple Salmon Taco Lettuce Wraps

This simple recipe is light and refreshing but filled with flavor. Reminiscent of traditional seaside Mexican cuisine, the healthy fats will keep you satisfied while the low-glycemic carbohydrates will provide antioxidants and fiber. Brighten these wraps up by squeezing fresh lime on top.

Serves 2

1 tablespoon avocado oil
1 pound wild salmon
Salt, to taste
Pepper, to taste
1 head butter lettuce
1 avocado, mashed
2 tablespoons Greek yogurt
2 tablespoons pico de gallo or salsa
1 lemon, cut in half

1. Heat the oil in a medium pan and add the salmon.

2. Add salt and pepper to taste, and cook over medium heat until cooked through, for about 8 to 10 minutes or until the internal temperature reaches 145°F. Break the salmon apart while cooking—leave the skin on or remove it as you wish.

3. Assemble the tacos by scooping the cooked salmon into individual lettuce cups and topping with your desired taco add-ons and freshly squeezed lemon juice.

Baked Whole Fish in Salt

A classic Italian dish, whole fish encrusted in salt is a simple way to prepare a delicate fillet of your favorite fish. Since the fish is whole with skin on, the salt merely locks in the flavor and moisture, without adding extra sodium. This dish pairs perfectly with roasted tomatoes and zucchini.

1 pound package coarse salt
1 whole white fish (1–1½ pounds)
2 tablespoons extra-virgin olive oil
Freshly squeezed juice from 3 lemons
2 teaspoons fresh mint, finely chopped

1. Preheat oven to 450°F.

2. Pour ⅓ package of salt on the bottom of a baking sheet with a surface area only slightly larger than the fish.

3. Place the whole fish on top of the salt layer and pour the rest of the salt over the fish until it is completely covered.

4. Place the baking sheet in the oven and roast for 25 to 30 minutes, depending on the weight of the fish.

5. Remove from oven and gently chip the salt away, then place the whole fish on a cutting board.

6. With a butter knife, gently scrape away the skin, and then take the fillet off the bone and plate. Flip the fish over and do the same on the other side.

7. Combine the extra-virgin olive oil, freshly squeezed lemon juice, and mint, and drizzle over the fillets.

Balsamic Slow-Cooker Chicken

Balsamic Slow-Cooker Chicken is as easy as adding the ingredients to your slow cooker and letting it do the work. This chicken can be used for a variety of meal ideas—lettuce-wrap tacos, a salad topper, or simply paired with your favorite vegetables.

Serves 4–6

1 teaspoon garlic powder
1 teaspoon dried basil
½ teaspoon pepper
2 teaspoons dried minced onion
8 boneless, skinless chicken thighs
1 tablespoon extra-virgin olive oil
4 garlic cloves, minced
½ cup balsamic vinegar
Sprinkle of fresh chopped parsley or cilantro

1. Combine the first four dry spices in a small bowl and season both sides of the chicken; set aside.

2. Pour olive oil and garlic on the bottom of the slow cooker and place chicken on top.

3. Pour balsamic vinegar over the chicken, cover, and cook on high for 4 hours.

4. Sprinkle fresh parsley or cilantro on top to serve.

Easy Pork Chop

This is a very simple preparation style that gives perfect flavor from an unlikely combination. The coconut oil gives the pork a subtle sweetness that is perfectly paired with a side of chilled sauerkraut. If you're not a fan of sauerkraut, coleslaw or roasted butternut squash are delicious complements to the pork.

Serves 1

2 tablespoons coconut oil
6-ounce pork chop
Salt, to taste
Pepper, to taste

1. In a medium skillet, melt the coconut oil over medium heat.

2. Season the pork chop with salt and pepper, to taste.

3. Place the pork in the skillet and cook for 4 to 5 minutes on each side, depending on thickness.

4. Cook to 145°F internal temperature (check with meat thermometer) or make an incision to make sure it is cooked through.

Caprese Turkey Burgers

If you like caprese salad, you'll love this turkey burger version of the tomato, basil, and mozzarella combination. This unique dish gives you the burger satisfaction while incorporating some fresh Italian flavors, and it pairs well with your favorite green vegetables.

Serves 1

6 ounces lean ground turkey
¼ teaspoon garlic powder
1 tablespoon almond flour
Pepper, to taste
2 slices mozzarella cheese
2 (½-inch) thick slices tomato
Handful of basil
2 tablespoons pesto sauce (store bought or homemade)

1. Combine ground turkey, garlic powder, almond flour, and pepper.

2. Form two patties.

3. Place patties on an aluminum foil–lined baking sheet. Broil on high for 3 minutes on each side.

4. Add one slice of mozzarella to the top of each burger at the last minute to melt.

5. Place burgers on a plate, and top each one with 1 tablespoon of pesto sauce, 1 tomato slice, and a handful of basil.

Creamy Crab-Stuffed Mushrooms

These Creamy Crab-Stuffed Mushrooms may strike you as a fancy appetizer at a party, but they are simple to make and, when paired with a side salad or green vegetables, your meal is complete. Feel free to use canned crab if you can't find it fresh, or if you prefer shrimp, the small bay variety works wonderfully in the dish.

Serves 4

20 ounces cremini mushrooms (20–25 individual mushrooms)

4 ounces cream cheese, softened to room temperature

4 ounces crabmeat, finely chopped

5 cloves garlic, minced

1 teaspoon dried oregano

½ teaspoon paprika

½ teaspoon black pepper

¼ teaspoon salt

2 tablespoons finely grated Parmesan cheese

1 tablespoon chopped chives or parsley

1. Preheat the oven to 400°F. Prepare a baking sheet lined with parchment paper.

2. Snap stems from mushrooms, discarding the stems and placing the mushroom caps on the baking sheet 1 inch apart from each other.

3. In a large mixing bowl, combine the cream cheese, crabmeat, garlic, oregano, paprika, pepper, and salt. Stir until well-mixed without any lumps of cream cheese.

4. Stuff the mushroom caps with the mixture. Evenly sprinkle Parmesan cheese on top of the stuffed mushrooms.

5. Bake until the mushrooms are very tender and the stuffing is nicely browned on top, about 30 minutes. Top with chives and serve while hot.

Beef and Broccoli Stir-Fry

You'll find all of the delicious traditional Asian flavors in this dish without the additional carbohydrates characteristic of typical noodles. This is a hearty dish, but if you're looking for something even more filling, feel free to serve over a bed of cooked cauliflower rice or shirataki noodles. If you have leftovers, you can use this beef-and-broccoli filling for delicious lettuce wraps.

Serves 2

¼ cup coconut aminos, divided

1 teaspoon fresh garlic, minced and divided

1 teaspoon fresh ginger, minced and divided

8 ounces flank steak, thinly sliced

1½ tablespoons avocado oil, divided

2½ cups broccoli, cut into large florets

¼ cup reduced-sodium beef broth

½ teaspoon sesame oil

Salt, to taste

Cooked cauliflower rice (optional)

Sesame seeds, for garnish

Green onion, for garnish

1. In a small bowl, whisk together 1 tablespoon of the coconut aminos, along with ½ teaspoon each of the garlic and ginger. Place the beef into the marinade and stir. Cover and refrigerate for at least 1 hour.

2. Heat 1 tablespoon of the oil in a large pan on medium heat. Add in the broccoli and cook, stirring frequently, until it just begins to soften, about 3 to 4 minutes. Add in the rest of the garlic and ginger and cook 1 minute.

3. Turn the heat to low, cover the pan, and cook until the broccoli is tender, about 4 to 5 minutes, stirring occasionally.

4. Once cooked, transfer the broccoli to a plate. Turn up the temperature to medium-high and add in the remaining ½ tablespoon of oil. Add in the marinated beef and cook until golden brown, about 2 to 3 minutes. Stir the broccoli back in.

5. In a small bowl, whisk together the rest of the coconut aminos, broth, and sesame oil. Pour it into the pan and cook until it begins to thicken, about 1 to 2 minutes, stirring constantly.

6. Season with salt, to taste.

7. Serve over cauliflower rice with green onion and sesame seeds (optional).

Honey-Mustard Salmon

Honey isn't typically allowed in the standard keto nutrition plan, but some people have an aversion to the flavor of salmon. If you're one of those people, this honey-mustard dish will allow you to reap all of the benefits of this nutritious fatty fish, as the honey mustard tends to balance out the salmon flavor.

Serves 3–4

1½ pounds salmon, skin removed, cut into 4 pieces
2 tablespoons whole-grain mustard (you can use regular mustard if you like)
2 tablespoons honey
1 clove garlic, minced
Juice of ½ a lemon

1. Preheat oven to 400°F.

2. Place salmon pieces on a sheet pan lined with parchment paper and bake for 10 minutes.

3. Meanwhile, in a small bowl, combine mustard, honey, garlic, and lemon juice.

4. After first 10 minutes of cooking, brush salmon with mixture and return to the oven for 5 minutes or until salmon is just cooked through.

Four-Ingredient Turmeric Scallops

Scallops may be thought of as an entrée in fancy seafood restaurant, but this simple four-ingredient dinner can be made in a matter of minutes. Scallops have a very mild seafood flavor and a hint of sweetness, making the perfect salad topper or partner for fresh vegetables.

Serves 2

1 tablespoon butter
½ pound fresh scallops
Turmeric, to taste
Juice of ½ lemon

1. Over medium heat, melt butter in a saucepan.

2. Add scallops and sprinkle with turmeric

3. Turn each scallop over after 3 to 4 minutes and sprinkle other side with turmeric.

4. Cook for 3 to 4 more minutes or until cooked through. Top with fresh lemon juice.

Meat Loaf Muffins

Meat Loaf Muffins are just like traditional meat loaf, except almond meal is used instead of a bread crumb filler. These mini versions can be made ahead of time and packed to be taken on the go or served warm with a side of roasted butternut squash.

Makes 12 Muffins

2 eggs
½ red bell pepper, diced
½ green bell pepper, diced
½ onion, diced
1½ pounds ground turkey, bison, or lean beef
½ cup tomato sauce
¾ cup almond meal
1 teaspoon garlic powder
Salt, to taste
Pepper, to taste
½ tablespoon extra-virgin olive oil, to grease muffin tins

1. In a large bowl, beat together eggs, bell peppers, and onion. Add ground meat, tomato sauce, almond meal, garlic powder, salt, and pepper; mix well with your hands until thoroughly combined.

2. Grease your muffin tin with oil. Separate meat loaf mixture into the tin and bake for 20 minutes or until meat loaf is done and passes the toothpick test.

Zucchini Lasagna Bolognese

This low-carbohydrate lasagna is still prepared similarly to the hearty favorite, using the same method but with zucchini strips instead of pasta. This filling dish will satisfy on its own or can be paired with a side salad, topped with Italian dressing.

Serves 5

1 pound zucchini (about 3 medium)

3 tablespoons extra-virgin olive oil, divided

Sea salt, to taste

4 cloves garlic, minced

2 pounds ground beef

2 cups tomato or spaghetti sauce

Pepper, to taste

12 ounces full-fat ricotta cheese

½ cup grated Parmesan cheese

1 large egg

3 cups mozzarella cheese, shredded

Fresh basil (optional)

1. Preheat the oven to 400°F. Line a large baking sheet with parchment paper.

2. Use a mandoline or knife to slice zucchini lengthwise into thin sheets, about ¼-inch thick.

3. Arrange the zucchini on the lined baking sheet, in a single layer. Brush both sides with olive oil (use about 2 tablespoons), then sprinkle both sides lightly with sea salt.

4. Roast the zucchini slices in the oven for 15 to 20 minutes, until soft and mostly dry.

5. When done, remove the zucchini from the oven. Pat the zucchini with paper towels to soak up any extra water or oil.

6. Heat the remaining tablespoon of oil in a sauté pan on the stove over medium-high heat. Add the garlic and sauté for 30 to 60 seconds, until fragrant.

7. Add the ground beef. Cook for about 10 minutes, until browned. Stir in the tomato or spaghetti sauce and remove from heat. Taste and add salt and pepper if needed.

8. Combine the ricotta and Parmesan cheeses. Stir in the egg.

9. Arrange a layer of zucchini slices at the bottom of a 9 x 13 glass casserole dish. Top with half of the meat sauce. Dollop small pieces of the ricotta cheese mixture, using half of the total amount, then spread. Finally top with half of the shredded mozzarella. Repeat the layers a second time, with shredded mozzarella last on top.

10. Bake for 15 minutes, until the cheese on top is melted and golden. Garnish with fresh basil, if desired.

Easy Baked Lemon-Butter Fish

If you are newer to seafood, this is a wonderful recipe to try, as it has a very mild fish taste—if you like chicken, you will probably enjoy this dish! Mild whitefish pairs well with steamed or sautéed green beans, with a generous amount of freshly squeezed lemon juice on top. To brighten it up even more, add some more fresh herbs in addition to the parsley.

Serves 4

¼ cup melted butter
4 garlic cloves, minced
Zest and juice of 1 lemon
2 tablespoons fresh parsley, minced, plus extra for serving
Salt, to taste
Pepper, to taste
4 fillets of cod, halibut, or rockfish
1 lemon, sliced

1. Preheat oven to 425°F.

2. In a bowl, combine the butter, garlic, lemon zest, lemon juice, and parsley; season with salt and pepper to taste.

3. Place the fish in a greased baking dish.

4. Pour the lemon butter mixture over the fish and top with fresh lemon slices.

5. Bake for 12 to 15 minutes, or until fish is flaky and cooked through.

6. Serve the fish topped with fresh parsley and freshly squeezed lemon juice.

Cheesy Chicken and Broccoli Casserole

Comfort food has never been this healthy! This warm and cheesy chicken-and-broccoli dish uses almond meal and cauliflower for filler, making it a low-carb rendition of your favorite casserole. This protein and vegetable dish has many components so it can be eaten on its own, or it does pair nicely with a crisp side salad.

Serves 4

Extra-virgin olive oil
1 cup cooked riced cauliflower
3 tablespoons almond meal
Your favorite seasonings
2 cups chicken broth (low sodium)
1 cup unsweetened almond milk
1 pound boneless skinless chicken breasts, chopped into bite size chunks
4 cups fresh broccoli florets
1½ cups of your favorite shredded cheese

1. Preheat oven to 400°F; using extra-virgin olive oil, grease a 13 x 9 inch baking dish.

2. Add cauliflower, almond meal, your favorite seasonings, chicken broth, and almond milk to the dish and whisk together.

3. Add the chicken and broccoli, stirring to distribute the chicken and broccoli into an even layer.

4. Cover and bake for 20 minutes.

5. Remove from the oven, add the cheese to the casserole and stir well to combine; return to the oven for 20 minutes, uncovered.

6. Remove once more, stir, and cook 20 minutes more until chicken is cooked through (total baking time is one hour).

Lamb Chops with Tzatziki

If you enjoy meats with a richer flavor, this traditional Greek lamb dish is typically served with tzatziki (cucumber yogurt sauce), and topped with freshly squeezed lemon juice. To pair with a Greek salad, simply chop some tomatoes, cucumber, and olives, and sprinkle with crumbled feta cheese and extra-virgin olive oil.

Serves 5

3 pounds lamb chops or 2 pounds lamb steaks
1 tablespoon extra-virgin olive oil
Rosemary, to taste
Salt, to taste
Pepper, to taste
Tzatziki Dipping Sauce (page 237)

1. Lightly coat the lamb chops or lamb steaks with olive oil, rosemary, salt, and pepper, and grill on each side for 6 to 9 minutes (for lamb steaks) or 2 to 4 minutes (for lamb chops), or until you have cooked through to your liking.

2. Plate the lamb and top with tzatkiki sauce.

Chapter 20

Almost Keto Side Dishes, Snacks, Dressings & Sauces

Whole Roasted Cauliflower

Serves 3

1 whole cauliflower
4 tablespoons butter
2 tablespoons extra-virgin olive oil
1 teaspoon garlic powder
3 tablespoons whole-grain mustard
Zest and juice of 1 lemon
½ teaspoon salt
½ teaspoon black pepper
¼ cup grated Parmesan cheese
Chopped parsley, to serve
Tahini, for dipping (optional)

1. Preheat oven to 425°F.

2. Trim the outer leaves of the cauliflower and trim the stalk so that it can stand upright on a baking dish.

3. Place the cauliflower on a parchment paper–lined baking tray or dish.

4. Melt the butter and mix with the extra-virgin olive oil.

5. Add the garlic powder, mustard, lemon zest and juice, salt, and pepper.

6. Brush the butter mixture all over the cauliflower.

7. Bake in the oven for 1 hour until tender, basting occasionally. Test it by inserting a skewer into the center of the cauliflower; it should pass through easily.

8. Remove from the oven, sprinkle with the Parmesan cheese, and place back into the oven for 5 minutes.

9. Sprinkle the chopped parsley over the cauliflower and serve with tahini to dip (optional).

Vegan Cashew Cheese Sauce

Makes 2 Cups

1½ cups raw cashew pieces
¼ cup nutritional yeast flakes
1 teaspoon salt
¼ teaspoon garlic powder
3 tablespoons freshly squeezed lemon juice
¾ cup water

1. In a food processor or blender, process the cashews into a fine powder, adding a drizzle of water if needed.

2. Add nutritional yeast, salt, and garlic powder, and process to combine.

3. Add lemon juice and water, and process until smooth.

Four-Ingredient Fish Dip

Makes 2 Cups

8 ounces smoked salmon
8 ounces crème fraîche
2 tablespoons freshly squeezed lemon juice
Fresh dill, to taste

1. Finely chop the smoked salmon and place in a medium bowl.

2. Add the crème fraîche and combine thoroughly until the mixture turns pink.

3. Add the lemon juice and mix.

4. Finely chop the dill and combine.

5. Serve cold with endive leaves or celery sticks.

Bone Broth

Serves 4

1 gallon water
2 tablespoons apple cider vinegar
2–4 pounds animal bones
Salt, to taste
Pepper, to taste

1. Place all ingredients in a large pot or slow cooker.

2. Bring to a boil.

3. Reduce to a simmer and cook for 12 to 24 hours. The longer it cooks, the better it will taste and more nutritious it will be.

4. Allow the broth to cool. Strain it into a large container and discard the solids.

Cauliflower Hummus

Serves 4

1 medium head cauliflower
4 tablespoons extra-virgin olive oil
½ cup tahini
2 garlic cloves
⅓ cup lemon juice
1 teaspoon salt
½ teaspoon ground black pepper
Chopped fresh parsley, to taste (optional)

1. Preheat oven to 375°F and chop cauliflower into small florets.

2. Toss cauliflower in extra-virgin olive oil and place on a baking sheet; roast until tender, about 20 minutes.

3. Place the roasted cauliflower in a food processor or blender and combine with all other ingredients.

Simply Steamed Artichoke

Serves 1–2

1 medium artichoke
1 teaspoon extra-virgin olive oil
Juice from 1 lemon
Avocado-oil mayo, for dipping

1. Bring a pot of water to a boil and, using a steaming rack, steam your artichoke until it's easy to pull out a leaf, about 30 minutes.

2. Plate and drizzle with extra-virgin olive oil and fresh lemon juice.

3. Use avocado-oil mayo for dipping.

Not Your Regular Brussels Sprouts

Serves 1

1 teaspoon extra-virgin olive oil
6 medium or large Brussels sprouts
Garlic powder, to taste
Black pepper, to taste
Freshly squeezed lemon juice

1. Heat extra-virgin olive oil in a pan over medium heat and evenly distribute the oil throughout the surface of the pan.

2. Place the Brussels sprouts flat-side down in the oil and sprinkle with garlic and black pepper.

3. Cook for 5 minutes or until the flat side of the sprouts are browned and turn the sprouts over to the round side. Add a bit more oil if needed.

4. Lower the heat to low and cook for 7 minutes with a cover over the pan.

5. Plate and top with freshly squeezed lemon juice.

Mashed Cauliflower

Serves 4

1 head cauliflower
½ cup grated Parmesan cheese

1. Chop cauliflower and steam until extremely tender.

2. Using a potato masher or fork, mash into a mashed potato–like texture.

3. Add grated Parmesan and thoroughly combine.

Parmesan Roasted Fennel

Serves 2

1 large fennel bulb, quartered and stems removed
1 tablespoon extra-virgin olive oil
2 tablespoons grated Parmesan cheese

1. Boil or steam the quartered fennel until tender; toss in extra-virgin olive oil

2. Roast for 10 minutes at 400°F; sprinkle with Parmesan cheese and roast for 2 minutes more.

Mushroom Stroganoff

Serves 6

Mushrooms:

4 cups mushrooms, sliced
3 cloves garlic, minced
½ yellow onion, thinly sliced
3 tablespoons extra-virgin olive oil
3 tablespoons tamari
¼ cup white wine

Stroganoff Sauce:

2 tablespoons extra-virgin olive oil
1 tablespoon sun-dried tomatoes
1 tablespoon paprika
½ cup vegetable stock
1 teaspoon black pepper
1 teaspoon rosemary
1 teaspoon thyme
½ cup cashews

For the Mushrooms:

1. Toss sliced mushrooms, garlic, and onion together in the olive oil and tamari. Set aside and marinate for 10 to 15 minutes.

2. Pan-cook mushroom mixture in a skillet over medium heat until tender; add wine and simmer for 5 minutes.

For the Sauce:

1. In a food processor or blender, combine all ingredients until smooth.

2. Transfer into the pan with mushrooms and continue to simmer until sauce thickens.

3. Serve on its own as a side dish or as a protein topping.

Creamy Cucumber Salad

Serves 2

½ cup plain almond or coconut yogurt
1 green onion, chopped
1 tablespoon red onion, sliced
Black pepper, to taste
1 tablespoon fresh dill, chopped, or ½
    teaspoon dried dill
1 garlic clove, minced
½ cup cucumber, thinly sliced

1. Combine yogurt with green onion, red onion, pepper, dill, and garlic.

2. Add cucumber slices and toss until evenly coated.

Kale Chips

Serves 2

3 cups curly kale
1 tablespoon extra-virgin olive oil
A few dashes of salt to taste

1. Preheat oven to 350°F.

2. Wash, dry, and chop kale into chip-sized pieces.

3. Drizzle extra-virgin olive oil over the kale and use your hands to evenly massage the oil into all leaves.

4. Bake for 10 to 12 minutes or until edges are lightly browned. Remove from the oven and lightly salt.

Tzatziki Dipping Sauce

Serves 4

1 cup Greek whole-milk yogurt
1 small cucumber, diced
2 cloves garlic, minced
2 tablespoons fresh lemon juice
2 tablespoons fresh dill, chopped (optional)
1 tablespoon fresh mint, finely chopped
   (optional)
Salt, to taste (optional)
Pepper, to taste (optional)

1. In a medium mixing bowl, combine all ingredients.

Fancy Cilantro and Basil Citrus

¼ cup chopped basil
¼ cup chopped cilantro
2 tablespoons lime juice
2 tablespoons orange juice
1 teaspoon honey
1 teaspoon grated ginger
½ teaspoon lime zest
Dash of pepper
2 tablespoons extra-virgin olive oil

1. Blend or puree all ingredients except extra-virgin olive oil.

2. Once those ingredients are blended, incorporate the oil using the blender or food processor.

Lemon Vinaigrette

¼ cup red wine vinegar
2 tablespoons Dijon mustard
1 clove garlic, minced
1 teaspoon dried oregano
¼ teaspoon ground black pepper
½ cup olive oil
2 tablespoons fresh lemon juice

1. Whisk red wine vinegar, mustard, garlic, oregano, and black pepper in a small bowl until blended.

2. Drizzle in oil, whisking until blended.

3. Beat lemon juice into the mixture.

Classic Vinaigrette

1 garlic clove
1 part balsamic vinegar
2 parts extra-virgin olive oil
Dash of honey
Black pepper to taste

1. Smash garlic clove with back of a knife and add to all other ingredients; whisk together.

Simple Dijon

1½ tablespoons white wine vinegar or cider vinegar
1 tablespoon Dijon mustard
1 lemon, juiced
1 shallot, diced

1. Combine all ingredients and whisk together.

Creamy Tahini-Honey Sauce

⅓ cup tahini
2 tablespoons water
1 tablespoon honey (or real maple syrup)

1. Mix tahini while slowly drizzling water until you reach your desired consistency.
2. Add the honey or maple syrup and combine.

Raspberry Vinaigrette

2 tablespoons raspberry vinegar
Freshly ground pepper, to taste
⅓ cup extra-virgin olive oil

1. Whisk vinegar and pepper in a small bowl. Slowly whisk in oil.

Smooth Tomato and Goat Cheese

¼ cup crumbled goat cheese
2 tablespoons white-wine vinegar
¼ cup extra-virgin olive oil
2 plum tomatoes, seeded and chopped
½ teaspoon salt
Freshly ground pepper, to taste
1 tablespoon chopped fresh tarragon
    (optional)

1. Blend all ingredients together until mixture is creamy and smooth. Makes one cup and can be refrigerated for up to three days.

Healthy Honey Mustard

1 clove garlic, minced
1 tablespoon white-wine vinegar
1½ teaspoons Dijon mustard (coarse or smooth)
½ teaspoon honey
Freshly ground pepper, to taste
⅓ cup extra-virgin olive oil

1. Whisk garlic, vinegar, mustard, honey, and pepper in a small bowl. Slowly whisk in oil.

Apple Cider Vinaigrette

1 part cider vinegar
1 part apple juice
2 parts extra-virgin olive oil
Black pepper, to taste
Cayenne pepper, to taste
Ground cinnamon, to taste

1. Whisk all ingredients together.

Lime and Cilantro Vinaigrette

1 cup packed cilantro
½ cup extra-virgin olive oil
¼ cup lime juice
¼ cup orange juice
½ teaspoon pepper
Pinch of minced garlic

1. Blend all ingredients together until mixture is creamy and smooth. Makes one cup and can be refrigerated for up to three days.

The Quick & Easy

2 parts extra-virgin olive oil
1 part balsamic vinaigrette
Your favorite seasonings

1. Whisk all ingredients together.

Asian Sesame Vinaigrette

¼ cup orange juice
¼ cup rice vinegar
2 tablespoons tamari
1 tablespoon toasted sesame oil
1 tablespoon honey or real maple syrup
1 teaspoon fresh ginger, finely grated

1. Blend all ingredients together until mixture is creamy and smooth. Makes ½ cup and can be refrigerated for up to seven days.

Creamy Cucumber Vinaigrette

1 small cucumber, peeled, seeded, and chopped
¼ cup extra-virgin olive oil
2 tablespoons red wine vinegar
2 tablespoons chopped fresh chives
2 tablespoons chopped fresh parsley
2 tablespoons Greek yogurt
1 teaspoon prepared horseradish (optional)

1. Blend all ingredients together until mixture is creamy and smooth.

Pesto

1½ cups fresh basil leaves (packed)
¼ teaspoon freshly ground black pepper
¼ cup freshly grated Parmigiano-Reggiano (optional)
2 tablespoons pine nuts or walnuts
1 teaspoon minced garlic
½ cup extra-virgin olive oil

1. Using a food processor or blender, combine the basil and pepper and process/blend for a few seconds until the basil is chopped.

2. Add the cheese, pine nuts, and garlic and while the processor is running, add the oil in a thin, steady stream until you have reached a smooth consistency.

Mango Salsa

1 mango, peeled and diced
½ cup cucumber, peeled and diced
1 tablespoon finely chopped jalapeño (optional)
⅓ cup diced red onion
1 tablespoon lime juice
⅓ cup roughly chopped cilantro leaves

1. Combine all ingredients and mix well.

Horseradish Cream Sauce

1 cup Greek yogurt
¼ cup grated fresh horseradish
1 tablespoon Dijon mustard
1 teaspoon white wine vinegar
¼ teaspoon freshly ground black pepper

1. Place all of the ingredients into a medium mixing bowl and whisk until the mixture is smooth and creamy.

2. Refrigerate for at least 4 hours to allow flavors to meld.

White Wine Sauce

½ cup chicken broth
¼ cup white wine
Juice of ½ lemon
1 tablespoon minced shallot
1 clove garlic, minced
1 tablespoon butter
1 tablespoon extra-virgin olive oil
Black pepper, to taste

1. Combine all ingredients in pan and use as a simmer sauce.

Chimichurri Sauce

1 bunch parsley, finely chopped
1 bunch cilantro, finely chopped
3 tablespoons capers, finely chopped
2 garlic cloves, minced
1½ tablespoons red wine vinegar
½ teaspoon red pepper flakes
½ teaspoon ground black pepper
½ cup extra-virgin olive oil

1. Put the parsley, cilantro, capers, and garlic in a medium mixing bowl and toss to combine.

2. Add the vinegar, red pepper flakes, and black pepper, and stir.

3. Pour in the olive oil and mix until well combined; let sit for 30 minutes so that the flavors blend.

Appendix A

Cooking Measurements Conversion Charts

Metric and Imperial Conversions

(These conversions are rounded for convenience.)

Ingredient	Cups/Table-spoons/Teaspoons	Ounces	Grams/Milliliters
Butter	1 cup/16 tablespoons/2 sticks	8 ounces	230 grams
Cheese, shredded	1 cup	4 ounces	110 grams
Cream cheese	1 tablespoon	0.5 ounce	14.5 grams
Cornstarch	1 tablespoon	0.3 ounce	8 grams
Flour, all-purpose	1 cup/1 tablespoon	4.5 ounces/0.3 ounce	125 grams/8 grams
Flour, whole wheat	1 cup	4 ounces	120 grams
Fruit, dried	1 cup	4 ounces	120 grams
Fruits or veggies, chopped	1 cup	5 to 7 ounces	145 to 200 grams
Fruits or veggies, pureed	1 cup	8.5 ounces	245 grams
Honey, maple syrup, or corn syrup	1 tablespoon	0.75 ounce	20 grams
Liquids: cream, milk, water, or juice	1 cup	8 fluid ounces	240 milliliters
Oats	1 cup	5.5 ounces	150 grams
Salt	1 teaspoon	0.2 ounce	6 grams
Spices: cinnamon, cloves, ginger, or nutmeg (ground)	1 teaspoon	0.2 ounce	5 milliliters
Sugar, brown, firmly packed	1 cup	7 ounces	200 grams
Sugar, white	1 cup/1 tablespoon	7 ounces/0.5 ounce	200 grams/12.5 grams
Vanilla extract	1 teaspoon	0.2 ounce	4 grams

US to Metric Conversions	
⅕ teaspoon	1 milliliter (ml)
1 teaspoon	5 ml
1 tablespoon	15 ml
1 fluid oz.	30 ml
⅕ cup	50 ml
1 cup	240 ml
2 cups (1 pint)	470 ml
4 cups (1 quart)	.95 liter
4 quarts (1 gal.)	3.8 liters
1 oz.	28 grams
1 pound	454 grams

Oven Temperatures		
FAHRENHEIT	CELSIUS	GAS MARK
225°	110°	1/4
250°	120°	1/2
275°	140°	1
300°	150°	2
325°	160°	3
350°	180°	4
375°	190°	5
400°	200°	6
425°	220°	7
450°	230°	8

Metric to US Conversions	
1 milliliter (ml)	⅕ teaspoon
5 ml	1 teaspoon
15 ml	1 tablespoon
30 ml	1 fluid oz.
100 ml	3.4 fluid oz.
240 ml	1 cup
1 liter	34 fluid oz.
1 liter	4.2 cups
1 liter	2.1 pints
1 liter	1.06 quarts
1 liter	.26 gallon
1 gram	.035 ounce
100 grams	3.5 ounces
500 grams	1.10 pounds
1 kilogram	2.205 pounds
1 kilogram	35 oz.

Measures for Pans and Dishes	
INCHES	CENTIMETERS
9-by-13-inches baking dish	22-by-33-centimeter baking dish
8-by-8-inches baking dish	20-by-20-centimeter baking dish
9-by-5-inches loaf pan (8 cups in capacity)	23-by-12-centimeter loaf pan (2 liters in capacity)

Appendix B

Calorie to Kilojoule Conversion Chart

CALORIES	KILOJOULES
1	4.1868
1,500	6,276
1,600	6,694
1,700	7,113
1,800	7,531
1,900	7,950
2,000	8,368
2,100	8,786
2,200	9,205
2,300	9,623
2,400	10,042
2,500	10,460

Acknowledgments

The information found in *Almost Keto* has been a joint passion of ours since 2011, and this book would not have been possible if it were not for the following people.

To our contributing writers, Dr. Kenneth Akey, Joy Giannaros, Katie Williams, and Jacqueline Cowan, your professional medical and nutritional expertise is unprecedented and so greatly appreciated.

Leah Zarra and Skyhorse Publishing, working with you has always been a pleasure. Your collaborative insight brings our nutrition information to life in every way we could have possibly hoped for.

Pamela Harty at the Knight Agency, thank you for believing in this project and for the last four years of your invaluable partnership.

To our families and friends, your ongoing support for our nutrition ventures has always been appreciated and encouraging.

Tim Hall, you were the catalyst who helped us decide to share our nutrition information, so thank you.

To our son's nanny, Marie Crosby, your ongoing care for our boy during hours away for work and writing has meant the world.

Our fantastic photographer, Marcel Boldu, and our talented makeup and hair stylist, Deisy Da Silva, thank you for your artistic finesse and for the fun day of photos.

And to Richard Oliva, Sr., (7/8/1935–10/24/2018) you are missed, and your memory lives on through Dorothy, your children, grandchildren, great-grandchildren, and the rest of your family.

About the Authors

Aimee Aristotelous, author of *The Whole Pregnancy*, is a certified nutritionist, specializing in ketogenic and gluten-free nutrition, as well as prenatal dietetics. Aristotelous is a contributing writer for a variety of publications including *Health, People, Yahoo! News, INSIDER, Motherly, Consumer Health Digest, Simply Gluten-Free, Well + Good, National Celiac Association*, and *Delight Gluten-Free*. She has appeared on the morning show in Los Angeles, as a regular speaker for the nationwide Nourished Festival, and has been the exclusive nutritionist for NBC affiliate KSEE 24 News California, appearing in more than fifty nutrition and cooking segments. Aimee has eight years of nutrition consulting experience and has helped over 2,000 people lose weight and get healthy!

Aimee's interest in nutrition began as she struggled with her own high cholesterol and weight gain after taking a sedentary office job in her twenties, once her athletic career came to an end. She furthered her nutrition education in the ketogenic and gluten-free realms after applying those dietary lifestyles to resolve her bad cholesterol, weight gain, and other dietary-related ailments such as migraine headaches. In addition to her Nutrition and Wellness certification through American Fitness Professionals and Associates, Aimee has a bachelor's degree in business/marketing from California State University, Long Beach. A California native, she currently resides in Fort Lauderdale, Florida, with her husband, Richard, and son, Alex, and enjoys the beach, cooking, and traveling.

Richard Oliva, coauthor of *The Eat to Keep Fit Diet*, is a certified nutritionist who specializes in ketogenic, gluten-free, and sports nutrition. He is a third-degree black belt in judo who has competed internationally and won state, national, and international titles. Oliva has conducted numerous nutrition seminars for colleges, health clubs, and medical practices, and has appeared in nutrition and cooking segments on NBC affiliate KSEE 24 News in California. He loves to share his lifetime passion for both nutrition and judo and has helped thousands of people learn how to eat better and improve their health and fitness.

Richard began studying nutrition at about the same time that he started learning judo in the mid-1970s, when he was in high school. He became a passionate student of nutrition after one of his coworkers at the time told him, "You know, you're killing yourself!" as Richard was eating a donut and drinking a soda during his break at his grocery store job. That comment launched him on a mission to learn everything he could about nutrition and health.

Richard earned his Nutrition and Wellness certification through American Fitness Professionals and Associates. He also has a Bachelor of Science degree in geology from Kent State University in Kent, Ohio. An Ohio native, he currently resides in Fort Lauderdale, Florida, with Aimee and Alex. Richard still enjoys practicing judo as well as weight training, cooking, and traveling.

Contributing Writers

Kenneth Akey, MD, FAAP

A graduate of the University of California, Irvine, School of Medicine, Dr. Kenneth Akey is a board-certified pediatrics doctor. In his twenty-five years of private practice, he has cultivated many strong relationships with his patients and their families. Dr. Akey's passions include developmental pediatrics and nutrition. He stresses the importance of a healthy diet to all of his patients and their parents, as they are often the ones with ultimate control over what their child eats. When Dr. Akey isn't providing warm, knowledgeable care for children, he enjoys working out, being involved at his church, and spending time with his wife, children, and grandchildren.

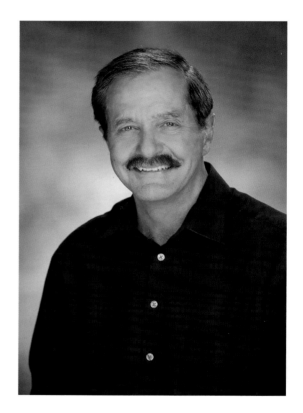

Joy Giannaros, Nutritional Therapist

Joy is vegan and a Nutritional Therapist who is keenly interested in the health benefits of plant-based nutrition. Joy used to struggle with alopecia, acne, and stubborn fat until she discovered the inseparable connection between diet and health. After seeing a radical transformation in her own skin, hair, and overall health, Joy began sharing her vegan experiences through her website (www.earthlingjoy.com) and Instagram page (@earthlingjoy). She has since helped many people lose weight, enjoy better health, and feel their very best. Joy holds a master's degree in Education from the University of Cambridge and has always upheld the importance of sharing knowledge as the most powerful tool for change in our lives. Previous to writing about plant-based nutrition, she was a school vice principal and continues to work part-time for the University of Cambridge in the Faculty of Education. Joy and her husband Joel are insatiable travelers and currently world-school their two rambunctious children: Ethan, an eight-year-old gregarious dude, and Sofia, a four-year-old avid fruitarian who has been vegan her whole life!

Photo by Joel Reid

Katie Munday Williams, RN BSN PHN

Katie Munday Williams graduated from the Johns Hopkins School of Nursing in 2004 and has worked in public health, surgery, pediatrics, and the NICU. She is passionate about educating patients on health- and nutrition-related topics and enjoys seeing people empower themselves to live healthy lifestyles. She is the owner of BabyMuse Sleep Consulting and recently became an International Board-Certified Lactation Consultant (IBCLC). In her free time, she enjoys playing piano, spending

Photo by Candy Coated Photography

time outdoors, and writing picture-book stories for children. Her first book, a biography of Anne Bradstreet, will be published in spring 2021. Katie lives in Santa Cruz, California, with her husband, Aaron, daughter, Rose, and son, James, where they enjoy gazing at hawks and raising caterpillars.

Jacqueline Cowan, PT, DPT

Dr. Jacqueline Cowan is a pelvic health and orthopedic physical therapist who practices in North County, San Diego. In 2010, she earned her doctoral degree in physical therapy from Boston University, one of the top-ranked PT schools in the country. She is passionate about providing wellness education, and encourages her patients to become happier, healthier, and stronger by promoting a healthy lifestyle. One of Jacqueline's main goals for herself is to keep abreast of the latest research and

Photo by Bryan Engel

treatment techniques by continually reading primary literature and taking courses to enhance her skills. In her free time, Jacqueline enjoys reading, jogging, Pilates, yoga, and walking on the beach with her husband, two daughters, and two rescue dogs.

References

L. E. James Abugoch, "Quinoa (Chenopodium quinoa Willd.): composition, chemistry, nutritional, and functional properties", *Advances in Food and Nutrition Research*, 58, 2009, 1–31. doi:10.1016/S1043-4526(09)58001-1 PMID 19878856

Adams, C., *Handbook of the Nutritional Value of Foods in Common Units* (New York: Dover Publications, 1986).

Arsenic and You: Information on Arsenic in Food, Water & Other Sources. Accessed May 21, 2019. https://www.dartmouth.edu/~arsenicandyou/index.html.

"Arsenic in Rice: Should You Be Concerned?" Healthline. Accessed May 21, 2019. https://www.health line.com/nutrition/arsenic-in-rice#section2.

Bentley, Jeanine. "U.S. Trends in Food Availability and a Dietary Assessment of Loss-Adjusted Food Availability, 1970–2014." USDA ERS, January 2017. https://www.ers.usda.gov/publications /pub-details/?pubid=82219.

"The Bill Clinton Vegan Diet." Holistic Holiday at Sea, n.d. http://holisticholidayatsea.com /the-bill-clinton-vegan-diet/.

Blau, JN, CA Kell, and JM Sperling. "Water-Deprivation Headache: A New Headache with Two Variants." NCBI. January 2004. Accessed May 23, 2019. https://www.ncbi.nlm.nih.gov/pubmed/14979888.

Brennan, Stuart. "Man City's Sergio Aguero Following Lionel Messi Diet Thanks to Martin Demichelis." *Manchester Evening News*, May 13, 2015. https://www.manchestereveningnews.co.uk/sport/football /football-news/man-citys-sergio-aguero-following-9239938.

"Calcium (Fact Sheet for Health Professionals)". Office of Dietary Supplements. National Institutes of Health. 2 March 2017. Archived from the original on 17 March 2018. Retrieved 17 March 2018.

Callegaro, D., and J. Tirapegui. "[Comparison of the Nutritional Value between Brown Rice and White Rice]." NCBI. October/November 1996. Accessed April 14, 2019. https://www.ncbi.nlm.nih.gov /pubmed/9302338.

Campbell, T. C., Thomas M. Campbell, and John Robbins. *The China Study*. Benbella Books, 2005.

Chinwong, S., D. Chinwong, and A. Mangklabruks. "Daily Consumption of Virgin Coconut Oil Increases High-Density Lipoprotein Cholesterol Levels in Healthy Volunteers: A Randomized Crossover Trial." NCBI. December 14, 2017. Accessed May 19, 2019. https://www.ncbi.nlm.nih.gov/pmc/articles /PMC5745680/.

Cousens, Gabriel. *Rainbow Green Live-Food Cuisine*. Berkeley, CA: North Atlantic Books, 2003, p. 56.

Damle, S. G. "Smart Sugar? The Sugar Conspiracy." NCBI. July 24, 2017. Accessed March 7, 2019. https://www.ncbi.nlm.nih.gov/pmc/articles/PMC5551319/.

Dashti, Hussein, Thazhumpal Mathew, Talib Hussein, Sami Asfar, Abdulla Behbahani, Mousa Khoursheed, Hilal Al-Sayer, Yousef Bo-Abbas, and Naji Al-Zaid. "Long-term Effects of a Ketogenic Diet in Obese Patients." NCBI. September/October 2004. Accessed March 30, 2019. https://www.ncbi.nlm.nih.gov/pmc/articles/PMC2716748/.

Farr, Gary, "Comparing Organic Versus Commercially Grown Foods." Rutgers University Study, New Brunswick, NJ, 2002.

Felman, Adam. "Does the Ketogenic Diet Work for Type 2 Diabetes?" Medical News Today. March 29, 2019. Accessed May 21, 2019. https://www.medicalnewstoday.com/articles/317431.php.

Furhman, J., Ferreri, D.M., "Fueling the vegetarian (vegan) athlete," *Current Sports Medicine Reports*, 9(4), July–August 2010, 233–241. doi:10.1249/JSR.0b013e3181e93a6f PMID 20622542

Fuhrman, J., and D.M. Ferreri. Fueling the vegetarian (vegan) athlete. *Curr. Sports Med. Rep.*, Vol. 9, No. 4, pp. 233Y241, 2010, p. 238.

Galland, L. "Diet and Inflammation." NCBI. December 2010. Accessed May 23, 2019. https://www.ncbi.nlm.nih.gov/pubmed/21139128.

Gostin, Lawrence O. "'Big Food' Is Making America Sick." NCBI. September 13, 2013. Accessed March 7, 2019. https://www.ncbi.nlm.nih.gov/pmc/articles/PMC5020160/.

Greger, Michael. *How Not to Die*. United Kingdom: Macmillan, 2016.

Griffin, BA. "Eggs: Good or Bad?" NCBI. August 1, 2016. Accessed April 6, 2019. https://www.ncbi.nlm.nih.gov/pubmed/27126575.

"Google Confirms the Plant-Based Revolution Is Coming." Rise of the Vegan, June 25, 2016. https://www.riseofthevegan.com/blog/google-confirms-the-plant-based-revolution-is-coming.

Hallberg L: Bioavailability of dietary iron in man. *Ann Rev Nutr* 1: 123-147, 1981.

Huang, RY., Huang, CC., Hu, F.B. et al. Vegetarian Diets and Weight Reduction: a Meta-Analysis of Randomized Controlled Trials, *Journal of General Internal Medicine*, 2016; vol 31, issue 1: 109—116. https://doi.org/10.1007/s11606-015-3390-7, accessed 5th May 2019.

Kaats, GR, D. Bagchi, and HG Preuss. "Konjac Glucomannan Dietary Supplementation Causes Significant Fat Loss in Compliant Overweight Adults." NCBI. October 22, 2015. Accessed May 20, 2019. https://www.ncbi.nlm.nih.gov/pubmed/26492494.

Kabara, J., D. Swieczkowski, A. Conley, and J. Truant. "Fatty Acids and Derivatives as Antimicrobial Agents." NCBI. July 1972. Accessed May 19, 2019. https://www.ncbi.nlm.nih.gov/pmc/articles/PMC444260/.

Kerstetter JE, O'Brien KO, Insogna KL. Low protein intake: the impact on calcium and bone homeostasis in humans. *J Nutr* 2003;133:855S-61S.

Kirkova, Deni. "Vegan Mr Universe, 40, Says Meat-Free Diet Has Made Him Stronger than Ever." *Metro*. Metro.co.uk, September 24, 2015. https://metro.co.uk/2015/09/24/vegan-body builder-40-aims-for-mr-universe-title-as-he-says-meat-free-diet-has-made-him-stronger-than-ever-5351168/.

Koller, VJ, M. Furhacker, A. Nersesyan, M. Misik, M. Eisenbauer, and S. Knasmueller. "Cytotoxic and DNA-damaging Properties of Glyphosate and Roundup in Human-derived Buccal Epithelial Cells." NCBI. May 2012. Accessed May 11, 2019. https://www.ncbi.nlm.nih.gov/pubmed/22331240.

Long, Cynthia (22 February 2012). "Crediting Tofu and Soy Yogurt Products"(PDF). Food and Nutrition Service (Memorandum). Alexandria, VA: United States Department of Agriculture. Archived from the original (PDF) on 12 July 2017. Retrieved 13 March 2018. "The Nutrition Standards in the National School Lunch and School Breakfast Programs final rule was published on January 26, 2012. The final rule gives schools the option to offer commercially prepared tofu as a meat alternate in the National School Lunch Program (NSLP) and School Breakfast Program (SBP)."

Malekinejad, H., and A. Rezabakhsh, "Hormones in Dairy Foods and Their Impact on Public Health—A Narrative Review Article," Hormones in Dairy Foods and Their Impact on Public Health—A Narrative Review Article, June 2015, accessed September 10, 2017, https://www.ncbi.nlm.nih.gov/pmc/articles/PMC4524299/.

Mangels, Reed, Messina, V., Messina M. *The Dietitian's Guide to Vegetarian Diets*. Sudbury, MA: Jones & Bartlett Learning, 2012, p. 75.

Mangels, R., *Vegetarian Journal*, volume XXVI, Issue 1, 2007. Accessed https://www.vrg.org/journal/vj2007issue1/vj2007issue1.pdf 10th April.

Maylon, Ed. "How a New Diet Has Helped Lionel Messi Turn around His Season." *Mirror*, May 11, 2015. https://www.mirror.co.uk/sport/football/news/bayern-munich-vs-barcelona-how-5677591.

Mayurama, K., T. Oshima, and K. Ohyama, "Exposure to exogenous estrogen through intake of commercial milk produced from pregnant cows," NCBI, February 2010, accessed September 10, 2017, https://www.ncbi.nlm.nih.gov/pubmed/19496976.

McNamara, Donald. "The Fifty Year Rehabilitation of the Egg." NCBI. October 2015. Accessed April 27, 2019. https://www.ncbi.nlm.nih.gov/pmc/articles/PMC4632449/.

Melina, V., Craig, W., Levin, S. Position of the academy of nutrition and dietetics: Vegetarian diets. *J. Acad. Nutr. Diet*. 2016, Volume 116, Issue 12, pp. 1970–1980.

Messina, L., and V. Messina, "The role of soy in vegetarian diets", *Nutrients*, 2(8), August 2010, 855–888. doi:10.3390/nu2080855PMID 22254060.

Michaëlsson, M., et al., "Milk intake and risk of mortality and fractures in women and men: cohort studies.," NCBI, October 28, 2014, accessed September 20, 2017, https://www.ncbi.nlm.nih.gov/pubmed/25352269.

Missimer, A., D. DiMarco, C. Andersen, A. Murillo, M. Vergara-Jiminez, and M. Fernandez. "Consuming Two Eggs per Day, as Compared to an Oatmeal Breakfast, Decreases Plasma Ghrelin While Maintaining the LDL/HDL Ratio." NCBI. February 01, 2017. Accessed April 27, 2019. https://www.ncbi.nlm.nih.gov/pmc/articles/PMC5331520/.

Mozaffarian, Dariush, Tao Hao, Eric Rimm, Walter Willett, and Frank Hu. "Changes in Diet and Lifestyle and Long-Term Weight Gain in Women and Men." *New England Journal of Medicine*. June 29, 2011. Accessed April 14, 2019. https://www.nejm.org/doi/full/10.1056/NEJMoa1014296.

Mumme, K., and W. Stonehouse. "Effects of Medium-chain Triglycerides on Weight Loss and Body Composition: A Meta-analysis of Randomized Controlled Trials." NCBI. February 2015. Accessed May 19, 2019. https://www.ncbi.nlm.nih.gov/pubmed/25636220.

Nestle, M. "Food Lobbies, the Food Pyramid, and U.S. Nutrition Policy." NCBI. July 1, 1993. Accessed February 16, 2019. https://www.ncbi.nlm.nih.gov/pubmed/8375951.

Niaz, K., E. Zaplatic, and J. Spoor. "Extensive Use of Monosodium Glutamate: A Threat to Public Health?" NCBI. March 19, 2018. Accessed May 11, 2019. https://www.ncbi.nlm.nih.gov/pmc/articles/PMC5938543/.

Ng, Marie, Tom Fleming, Margaret Robinson, Blake Thomson, Nicholas Graetz, and Christopher Margano. "Global, Regional, and National Prevalence of Overweight and Obesity in Children and Adults during 1980–2013: A Systematic Analysis for the Global Burden of Disease Study 2013." *The Lancet*. May 28, 2014. Accessed February 06, 2019. https://www.thelancet.com/journals/lancet/article/PIIS0140-6736(14)60460-8/fulltext.

Nutrition Facts Label: Total Carbohydrates, FDA. Accessed on 16th of April 2019, from: https://www.accessdata.fda.gov/scripts/inter activenutritionfactslabel/factsheets/Total_Carbohydrate.pdf

Oyebode O, Gordon-Dseagu V, Walker A, et al. Fruit and vegetable consumption and all-cause, cancer and CVD mortality: analysis of Health Survey for England data. *J Epidemiol Community Health* 2014;68:856-862.

Paoli, Antonio. "Ketogenic Diet for Obesity: Friend or Foe?" NCBI. February 01, 2014. Accessed March 23, 2019. https://www.ncbi.nlm.nih.gov/pmc/articles/PMC3945587/.

Parker, John. "The Year of the Vegan." *The Economist*. https://worldin2019.economist.com/theyearofthevegan?utm_source=412&utm_medium=COM.

Pase, CS, et al., "Influence of perinatal trans fat on behavioral responses and brain oxidative status of adolescent rats acutely exposed to stress.," NCBI, September 05, 2013, accessed September 02, 2017, https://www.ncbi.nlm.nih.gov/pubmed/23742847.

Percival, Mark. "Nutritional Support for Connective Tissue Repair and Wound Healing." *Clinical Nutrition Insights*, 1997, 1–4. Accessed May 23, 2019. https://acudoc.com/Injury Healing.PDF.

Pross, N., A. Demazieres, N. Girard, R. Barnouin, F. Santoro, E. Chevillotte, A. Klein, and L. Le Bellego. "Influence of Progressive Fluid Restriction on Mood and Physiological Markers of Dehydration in Women." NCBI. January 28, 2013. Accessed May 23, 2019. https://www.ncbi.nlm.nih.gov/pubmed/22716932.

Samsel, A., and S. Seneff. "Glyphosate, Pathways to Modern Diseases II: Celiac Sprue and Gluten Intolerance." NCBI. December 2013. Accessed May 11, 2019. https://www.ncbi.nlm.nih.gov/pmc/articles/PMC3945755/.

Santarelli, RL, F. Pierre, and D. Corpet. "Processed Meat and Colorectal Cancer: A Review of Epidemiologic and Experimental Evidence." NCBI. March 25, 2008. Accessed April 14, 2019. https://www.ncbi.nlm.nih.gov/pmc/articles/PMC2661797/.

Singh, N., "Essential fatty acids, DHA and human brain.," NCBI, March 01, 2005, accessed September 05, 2017, https://www.ncbi.nlm.nih.gov/pubmed/15812120.

Snyder, Kimberly. *The Beauty Detox Solution*. Harlequin Enterprises (Australia) Pty, Limited, 2011.

Soffritti, M., M. Padovani, E. Tibalidi, L. Falcioni, F. Manservisi, and F. Belpoggi. "The Carcinogenic Effects of Aspartame: The Urgent Need for Regulatory Re-evaluation." NCBI. April 2014. Accessed April 14, 2019. https://www.ncbi.nlm.nih.gov/pubmed/24436139.

"Statistics About Diabetes: Overall Numbers, Diabetes and Prediabetes." Www.diabetes.org. Accessed May 21, 2019. http://www.diabetes.org/diabetes-basics/statistics/.

Swithers, S. "Artificial sweeteners produce the counterintuitive effect of inducing metabolic derangements," NCBI, September 2013, accessed September 24, 2017, https://www.ncbi.nlm.nih.gov/pmc/articles/PMC3772345/.

Tick, H. "Nutrition and Pain." NCBI. May 2015. Accessed May 23, 2019. https://www.ncbi.nlm.nih.gov/pubmed/25952067.

Tonstad S, Butler T, Yan R, Fraser GE. Type of vegetarian diet, body weight, and prevalence of type 2 diabetes. *Diabetes Care*. 2009;32(5):791–6.

Towery, P., JS Guffey, C. Doerflein, K. Stroup, S. Saucedo, and J. Taylor. "Chronic Musculoskeletal Pain and Function Improve with a Plant-based Diet." NCBI. October 2018. Accessed May 23, 2019. https://www.ncbi.nlm.nih.gov/pubmed/30219471.

"Type 2 Diabetes." Centers for Disease Control and Prevention. August 15, 2018. Accessed February 16, 2019. https://www.cdc.gov/diabetes/basics/type2.html.

U.S. Trends in Food Availability and a Dietary Assessment of Loss-Adjusted Food Availability, 1970–2014, Accessed on April 16, 2019, from https://www.ers.usda.gov/publications/pub-details/?pubid=82219.

Vega-Gálvez, A., et al., "Nutrition facts and functional potential of quinoa (Chenopodium quinoa willd.), an ancient Andean grain: a review", *Journal of the Science of Food and Agriculture*, 90(15), December 2010, 2541–2547. doi:10.1002/jsfa.4158 PMID 20814881.

Walsh, S. *Plant Based Nutrition and Health*. Birmingham, UK: The Vegan Society, 2012.

Wasserman, D., and R. Mangels, *Simply Vegan*, 5th Edition 2013, published by The Vegetarian Resource Group, Baltimore. 2018 revisions accessed from https://www.vrg.org/nutrition/iron.php on 3rd May.

Zhang, G., A. Pan, G. Zhong, Z. Yu, H. Wu, X. Chen, L. Tang, Y. Feng, H. Zhou, H. Li, B. Hong, WC Willett, VS Malik, D. Spiegelman, FB Hu, and X. Lin. "Substituting White Rice with Brown Rice for 16 Weeks Does Not Substantially Affect Metabolic Risk Factors in Middle-aged Chinese Men and Women with Diabetes or a High Risk for Diabetes." NCBI. September 01, 2011. Accessed April 14, 2019. https://www.ncbi.nlm.nih.gov/pubmed/21795429.

Index